The Joe Aldrich LIFE-STYLE EVA

JOE ALDRICH
Life Style
EVANGELISM
N A T U R A L L Y

LIBERATING YOUR WITNESS IN YOUR WORLD. NATURALLY.

1 WHEN PEOPLE SEE THE LIGHT
Our mission is to make visible the invisible God.

2 BREAKING THROUGH THE CULTURAL BARRIER
We're called to love—and love demands contact and association.

3 TAKING THE PULSE OF A GROWING CHURCH
God is looking for churches that qualify for His blessing.

4 BECOMING A REDEMPTIVE NEIGHBOR
You've got something that can nudge your neighbors to the Cross.

Available at your local film library
Other Life-Style Evangelism Training Tools from Multnomah Press

THE LISTENING GUIDE:
A booklet designed to help groups and individuals get sustained benefit from each of the four Life-Style Evangelism films. Includes case studies and questions for discussion. $1.95

THE BOOK:
Life-Style Evangelism by Joe Aldrich. A "Critical Concern" best seller on how to cross traditional boundaries to reach the unbelieving world.

THE STUDY GUIDE:
The companion guide for in-depth study and application of the Life-Style Evangelism book. $2.95

THE CASSETTE SERIES:
Hear Joe Aldrich's teaching on life-style evangelism, recorded in a set of six tape cassettes. $39.95

Multnomah Productions
Portland, Oregon 97266

Books in the Critical Concern series:

- Abortion: Toward An Evangelical Consensus
- Beyond Hunger: A Biblical Mandate for Social Responsibility
- Birthright: Christian, Do You Know Who You Are?
- Christian Countermoves in a Decadent Culture
- The Christian Mindset in a Secular Society: Promoting Evangelical Renewal and National Righteousness
- The Christian, the Arts, and Truth: Regaining the Vision of Greatness
- Christians in the Wake of the Sexual Revolution: Recovering Our Sexual Sanity
- The Church & the Parachurch: An Uneasy Marriage
- The Controversy: Roots of the Creation-Evolution Conflict
- The Cosmic Center: The Supremacy of Christ in a Secular Wasteland
- Culture in Christian Perspective: A Door to Understanding and Enjoying the Arts
- Death and the Caring Community: Ministering to the Terminally Ill
- Decision Making and the Will of God: A Biblical Alternative to the Traditional View
- Depression: Finding Hope & Meaning in Life's Darkest Shadow
- Imagination: Embracing a Theology of Wonder
- Liberated Traditionalism: Men & Women in Balance
- Life-Style Evangelism: Crossing Traditional Boundaries to Reach the Unbelieving World
- The Majesty of Man: The Dignity of Being Human
- The Trauma of Transparency: A Biblical Approach to Inter-personal Communication
- Worship: Rediscovering the Missing Jewel

Life-Style Evangelism

Crossing Traditional Boundaries to Reach the Unbelieving World

JOSEPH C. ALDRICH

MULTNOMAH PRESS
PORTLAND, OREGON 97266

Cover design and illustration: Britt Taylor Collins

LIFE-STYLE EVANGELISM
© 1981 by Multnomah Press
Portland, Oregon 97266

Printed in the United States of America

Library of Congress Cataloging in Publication Data

Aldrich, Joseph C   1940-
   Life-style evangelism.

   Includes indexes.
   1. Evangelistic work.   2. Witness bearing (Christianity)
I. Title.
BV3790.A48   253.7   80-27615
ISBN 0-930014-46-4 (hdbk.)
ISBN 0-88070-023-8 (pbk.)

        87   88   89   90   –   11   10   9   8

To Roland Niednagel,
a dear brother and fellow evangelist
whose continued encouragement
prompted the writing of this book

Read This First

I am a skeptic.

Not along the lines of the French skeptic Voltaire, or the Scottish philosopher and historian David Hume, or even the German idealist Immanuel Kant, who were all skeptical about the ability of man, using his reason, to know anything with certainty. But, in the broader sense of the word, I am a skeptic in that I possess a questioning attitude about certain subjects. Especially when it comes to challenging traditional and conventional beliefs to which I dearly cling. (Even though these beliefs may be unscriptural.)

I started reading this book with great hesitation. My personal life wasn't the epitome of evangelistic effectiveness, but I did have my favorite collection of Bible verses which proved: (1) the world would always be hostile to the message of Jesus Christ, (2) not many enter the Kingdom, (3) the command to evangelize is somewhat restricted in its application, and, most importantly, (4) I probably don't have "the gift." Little did I know that the author of this book would challenge those dearly held beliefs with entire sections of Scripture where God exhorts us to follow His Son and His Son's disciples—across the street, next door, into the rest of the world— and take His love and His message of hope as our calling cards.

Rather than write about how my overall view of evangelism has been changed through interacting with the message of this book, I prefer to let a few (of whom there are many) speak about the author's ideas. "A few" include a businessman, a pastor and his wife, and a housewife. The first is Lou Purmort, Founder and Vice-Chairman of U. S. Filter Corporation, a "Fortune 500" company located in Newport Beach, California.

"Joe Aldrich has been the most meaningful person in my life. Why? I became a born again Christian on August 20, 1972, by accepting Jesus Christ as my personal Savior—and that event occurred in Joe's office after his suggestion that I should trust Christ. Ever since Joe has taken me—probably the worst of all sinners—and loved me into a personal relationship with Jesus Christ, I have lived an entirely new and 'abundant life' (John 10:10).

"Before becoming a Christian, I thought I had everything: family, good health, three houses, six boats, four cars, and a successful business. But even with all of these good things, something was still missing inside. Since 1972, I know the real meaning of life, and that is life in Christ. And I would gladly trade all my materialistic things for the relationship with God I now have.

"Joe was there to share and listen when I needed him. And from my personal experience, I can truly say Joe practices what he preaches."

Joe's biblical philosophy of evangelism has not only helped businessmen, but it has also helped pastors. Gary Cassady, Associate Pastor of Northwest Hills Baptist Church in Corvallis, Oregon, tells how.

"My wife and I attended the conference for pastors in Colorado where Joe Aldrich was the speaker. At that conference we accepted the challenge to begin praying for at least five couples in our neighborhood. We had previously made contact with a number of them, but had not really prayed much for them. We actually had not been ready 'to give an answer for the hope that is within us.'

"Since the time of that conference, God has given us some amazing opportunities. One of the most exciting is a relationship which is developing with a family that moved here from Chile. My wife has been meeting

with his wife each Wednesday afternoon for some time now, helping her to learn English by reading the Bible. She and her husband are deeply appreciative, and, what's more, they have begun to ask a number of questions related to spiritual things.

"I have challenged the students in my high school class to write on a bookmark in their Bible the names of people for whom they will pray and be available 'neighbors.' Three weeks ago a brother of one gal in the class and the woman he was living with both made a commitment to Christ. They have now begun attending our church. We're excited at what God is doing!"

Families have also been affected by Dr. Aldrich and his wife Ruthe. This final narrative by Linda Slocum of Richardson, Texas, is a good summary of the kind of life-changing influence God has had through them.

"Seventeen years ago I moved into a lovely apartment with a load of dreams. My dental student husband was in his senior year and we had decided to treat ourselves to luxuries—a swimming pool and a dishwasher —for the last few months before his graduation. I dreamed of soon quitting my secretarial job and starting a family. But all my dreams exploded just a few weeks later when my husband moved out and filed for a divorce. When the rent was due that month, I revealed my tragedy to the managers of the apartment only because we had rented it on a special discount for dental students and the dental student was gone. The managers happened to be a couple, a seminary student and a school teacher, named Joe and Ruthe Aldrich.

"Ruthe empathized with the heartache and loneliness I felt; she genuinely seemed to care. She told me that she believed her own marriage worked because she and Joe put Christ at the center of it. I didn't understand, but it sure sounded good.

"Ruthe stopped by often to check on me, and over the next days and weeks, she and Joe began to take me out to dinner and have me over for meals. As they opened their lives to me, I knew I had found some very special friends, unlike any I'd ever known. They always seemed to care and have time to listen to me and even cry with me. From the close vantage point they gave me of their lives, I knew there was something about them and their marriage that I truly wanted. The books and Bible verses they gave me were wrapped in their constant love. Eventually I asked them about their personal relationship to Christ. It was so simple and clear for me when they came to Revelation 3:20 that I had no doubt what my response was to be. That night I invited Christ into my life.

"Though I had hoped that my problems would be over the next day, they weren't. My marriage never mended and I struggled over my future. But I knew that I was a new creature and had been given a fresh start in life by Christ. The constant support and encouragement of Ruthe and Joe kept me going. As they helped me discover what was happening to me, I began to see God's Spirit at work in my life and I wanted to share what I'd found with others. As I studied and learned how to do just that, I also knew that I needed to get involved in people's lives and learn to love and care for them—just like the Aldriches had loved and cared for me.

"That spring and summer, around the swimming pool, the three of us spent time getting better acquainted with our neighbors. People opened up to us with questions about our personal faith when we took the time to invite them over for hamburgers. Several made quiet commitments to Christ during the course of the Bible study Joe taught at my apartment. I could go on and on.

"I am now married to a wonderful Christian man and have a six-year old son. Our thirteen-year mar-

riage has not been problem-free, but God has helped us work through the difficulties as I've practiced Joe and Ruthe's plan—putting Christ at the center of our marriage. As we have learned to communicate this reality of our faith to others, God continues to bring us back to the same costly kind of evangelism Ruthe and Joe used to minister to me: mixing the Good News with genuine love, care, and friendship."

Joe Aldrich would disclaim any credit for the above stories, other than that he does believe in being available to be used by God in people's lives. And this is the pattern set before us by Jesus Christ in His earthly life.

My cold skepticism has melted into a warm and enthusiastic belief in this book's principles. Biblically and practically, I have been convinced. And because of this book's encouragement, I have gotten across the street and next door to meet—and become involved with—my neighbors.

If you are concerned about evangelism, if you are concerned about people, if you are concerned about God's plan for men on earth . . . give this book a fair reading. You may change your views—as I did.

And then, quite possibly, God can use you in the lives of those who are skeptical about Christianity. So that they will believe.

John Sloan, Th.M.
Editor, Multnomah Press

Foreword

If Jesus appeared on earth today as He did 2000 years ago, many churches would not elect Him to their official boards. He would have disqualified Himself because He ran with the wrong crowd.

The historian Luke comments that tax collectors and sinners —folks shunned by religious types because they had made a mess of life—kept seeking Him out to hear what He had to say. When they came to Him, Jesus gave them a hearty welcome and often enjoyed dinner with them. Socializing with people like that ruined His testimony. The Pharisees and Bible teachers who observed Him wrote off His association with that element of society as a secret sympathy with sin. Yet, the fact remains Jesus went out of His way to cultivate those relationships, and if we are serious about following Him, we must do the same thing.

Making a place in your life for non-Christian neighbors demands effort, thought, and at times risk. Bridges are harder to construct than walls. But that doesn't alter this reality: Outsiders to faith are first drawn to Christians and then to Christ. Unfortunately, not all Christians attract. Like a turned magnet, some repel. Yet Christians, alive to God, loving, caring, laughing, sharing, involved at the point of people's need, present an undeniable witness for Christ in their society.

Developing a life style to make that happen is what this book is all about. That is why thoughtful Christians will read it, and that is why neighbors who live next door or share a ride with us or work with us may thank God we did.

Dr. Haddon W. Robinson
President, Denver Conservative Baptist Seminary

11

Contents

Introduction

The Enterprise Called Evangelism

*T*here is a legend which recounts the return of Jesus to glory after His time on earth. Even in heaven He bore the marks of His earthly pilgrimage with its cruel cross and shameful death. The angel Gabriel approached Him and said, "Master, you must have suffered terribly for men down there."

"I did," He said.

"And," continued Gabriel, "do they know all about how you loved them and what you did for them?"

"Oh, no," said Jesus, "not yet. Right now only a handful of people in Palestine know."

Gabriel was perplexed. "Then what have you done," he asked, "to let everyone know about your love for them?"

Jesus said, "I've asked Peter, James, John, and a few more friends to tell other people about Me. Those who are told will in turn tell still other people about Me, and My story will be spread to the farthest reaches of the globe. Ultimately, all of mankind will have heard about My life and what I have done."

Gabriel frowned and looked rather skeptical. He knew well what poor stuff men were made of. "Yes," he said, "but what if Peter and James and John grow weary? What if the people who come after them forget? What if way down in the twentieth century, people just don't tell others about you? Haven't you made any other plans?"

And Jesus answered, "I haven't made any other plans. I'm counting on them."

Twenty centuries later . . . He still has no other plan. He's counting on you and me. High on God's "To Do" list is the evangelization of the world. His early disciples adopted His priorities and devoted themselves to reaching their world. Christ counted on them, and they delivered. Have we done as well?

TOO MANY PEOPLE

Before we succumb to another "guilt trip," let's consider some reasons why we appear "ineffective" when compared to the apostles. Our purpose is not to excuse ourselves. But clearly we need to understand some of the forces or influences which hinder our effectiveness.

First, the need to relate to the ever-increasing number of people in our daily experience has crippled our ability to relate effectively to even one person. *Excessive relational demands have crippled our relational capacities.* There are simply too many people. A casual stroll down the street brings me face to face with dozens of people every minute. I cannot possibly recognize or relate to them. I must pass by them and treat them as indifferently as parts of machinery moving down an assembly line. To make matters worse, population densities of most metropolitan areas reinforce alienation and indifference.

This attitude of isolation becomes a way of life. I don't want to bother you, and I don't want you to bother me. Am I my brother's keeper? By all means—No! Unable to relate to the hordes of people, my mind concludes that there are no people. Asia's teeming millions don't exist. "What people? I don't see any people." One million people become zero.

This response of unconcern may be necessary to maintain some sort of psychological equilibrium. But it certainly hurts the evangelistic enterprise. At the times when relationship is critical to the gospel's impact, we discover that most Christians have neither significant contacts with non-Christians nor the ability to relate in a redemptive manner. When it comes to relating to people, we find that bigness is not necessarily best.

STOP THE WORLD—I CAN'T GET OFF

A second reason for ineffectiveness is *the pace of life: It is too fast and complicated*. Technological acceleration has directly affected our way of living. Jobs change, people move, congestion grows, traffic jams. Telephones ring incessantly, and the TV drones on and on whether watched or not. Held captive by schedules and the demands of others, we find ourselves unable to slow our world and get off.

Add to this swift pace the complexities of our world's problems. We live under the threat of momentary annihilation. News reports of crises around the world and next door jam our mental capacities beyond their load limit. We are inundated with problems beyond our comprehension and sense that no one has the solution.

Caught up in a whirlwind of activity, schedules, and events, we find that healthy, supportive, "people" time is an increasingly rare commodity. Adding evangelism to an already hectic schedule would certainly be the straw that would break the camel's back.

AQUARIUMS, AMBUSHES, AND SAFARIS

A third source of ineffectiveness in evangelism is *our exposure to unhealthy evangelism models*. The evangelism "options" as presented and practiced only provide realistic opportunities for a small percentage of the Christian community. Although many of the evangelism practices "work," in some cases they actually hinder the total impact of a given church in a community. While some churches fail to grow because they do not evangelize, others fail to grow because they do—but in outmoded, ineffective forms.

For many, evangelism is what the pastor does on Sunday morning as he throws the lure over the pulpit, hoping some "fish" in the stained-glass aquarium will bite. The "layman's" job is simply to herd fish within the reach of the "big fisherman." Week after week the pastor evangelizes the evangelized. His people will grow weak on a diet of evangelistic sermons, unable to witness effectively about the reality of the full-orbed gospel in their own lives. The starved church members "are unable to witness to the good news . . . (because) they are not experiencing it."[1] It is a strange phenomenon indeed for a church group whose major emphasis is evangelism.

The truth is that "everything that happens, teaches." If the only means of evangelism is the "big fisherman" who continually fishes from the pulpit, he may catch some; but he is really teaching by his actions an approach to evangelism which may hinder the evangelistic potential of his local fellowship. Evangelism is contextual, and without careful attention to the "beauty of the body" (edification), evangelistic efforts become increasingly contrived, unnatural, and ineffective. Effective individual evangelism grows out of the context of a healthy, vibrant fellowship of believers (church). The impact of its evangelistic efforts are directly proportional to the health of its corporate life.

Another potentially unhealthy evangelism model is what I call the "ambush method." The non-Christian is invited to an event where a high-powered speaker unloads both barrels. Often the "guest" has no idea of the function or purpose of the invitation and feels trapped and embarrassed. This method reminds some of sawdust trails or scalding tears fueled by people skilled in manipulation of both emotions and Scripture.

Many assume that evangelism is what Billy Graham does and thus remove themselves from involvement because they "don't have his gifts." Sometimes the only exposure to evangelism for believers is being part of a weekly task force on a "spiritual safari" into enemy territory. On such forays total strangers are confronted with a verbal message said to be the gospel. Some such experiences of evangelism are valid, and God blesses. Many are not, though, and represent an unbalanced, unnatural, and, in some cases, unbiblical approach to reaching people.

I find that many believers have been burned by an unfortunate—and often unnecessary—experience of attempting to evangelize someone. As a result they have given up. Often this bad experience is the result of a failure to distinguish between witnessing and soul winning. Yet there are differences between these two terms. "As long as a man simply tells another ABOUT Jesus, he is a witness. But the moment he tries to get that person to DO SOMETHING with Christ, he shifts over to the role of the soul winner."[2] Witnessing and soul winning are two different specialties. Many have been taught that evangelism equals soul winning, and have tried "soul winning" with disastrous results. Embarrassed and humiliated, they have withdrawn themselves completely from anything to do with evangelism. I might add that true witnessing is based on what we (the saved) do which they (the unsaved) cannot do, not upon what we don't do which they do.

Because of exposure to unhealthy evangelism models, the evangelism enterprise has been hurt. Often it is the methodology of some of these models which offends the sensitivities of caring Christians. Sometimes they are artificial and unnatural. Many Christians have personal objections to some of the approaches to "winning" the lost. Gimmicks, pseudo-questionnaires, buttonholing, evangelical mugging, and the outright rudeness of some witnesses turn them off. The end result is that evangelism becomes a much misunderstood term; one which most people either swear by . . . or at.

SEPARATION OR SEGREGATION

Perceived cultural barriers and outright theological errors combine to make the fourth ineffective factor which short-circuits evangelism. I think it is fair to say that the majority of Christians have lost their ability to relate significantly to non-Christians. By no stretch of the imagination can the Christian community be called the "salt of the earth."

For salt to be effective, it must get out of its container and into the world of hurting, dying, suffering, sinning people. There is no impact without contact, and yet, after knowing the Lord two years, the average Christian has no significant relationships with non-Christians. Often conversion opens up a whole new web of relationships and the new Christian inadvertently drifts away from his non-Christian associates. In some cases the nature of his past associations makes separation a necessity if growth is to take place. All too often, however, he withdraws from significant contact because his local church misunderstands the biblical doctrine of separation.

Frequently the unsaved are viewed as enemies rather than victims of the Enemy. Spirituality is viewed as separation from the unsaved. The new Christian is told he has "nothing in common" with his unsaved associates. Quite frankly, I have a lot in common with them: a mortgage, car payments, kids who misbehave, a lawn to mow, a car to wash, a less-than-perfect marriage, a few too many pounds around my waist, and an interest in sports, hobbies, and other activities they enjoy. It is well to remember that Jesus was called a "friend of sinners." A *friend* of sinners. Selah!

BRIDGING THE CREDIBILITY GAP

A fifth cause of a weakened evangelistic enterprise is the imbalance between the verbalization and the incarnation of the gospel. Christians are to *be* good news before they *share* the good news. The words of the gospel are to be incarnated before they are verbalized. Let me put it another way. The music of the gospel must precede the words of the gospel and prepare the context in which there will be a hunger for those words.

What is the music of the gospel? The *music* of the gospel is the beauty of the indwelling Christ as lived out in the everyday relationships of life. The *gospel* is the good news that Jesus Christ has solved the problem of man's sin and offers him the potential of an exchanged life, a life in which the resources of God Himself are available for his transformation. And as the gospel is translated into music, it makes redemptive relationships possible. When the world observes husbands loving their wives, and wives supporting and caring for their husbands and families, they have seen a miracle; they have heard the music. It is miraculous music for which many of them are longing.

The two greatest forces in evangelism are a healthy church and a healthy marriage. The two are interdependent. You can't have one without the other. It is the healthy marriage, however, which is the "front lines weapon." The Christian family in a community is the ultimate evangelistic tool, assuming the home circle is an open one in which the beauty of the gospel is readily available. It's the old story: *When love is seen, the message is heard*.

Even God's evangelism strategy in the Old and New Testament involves a beautiful bride and her relationship to Him. Israel and the church are called "brides" by God and their beauty is of great concern to Him. But the beauty described (Ezekiel 16, Ephesians 5) is relational. It is the beauty of how they lived together. Israel became a harlot because she forgot the source of her beauty and splendor. The church at Ephesus was charged with the loss of beauty even though she was theologically sound (the condition of hundreds of churches today).

Most evangelism training involves helping people learn how to "say the words" of the gospel. Little attention is paid to developing a biblical philosophy of ministry which moves the corporate life of the church away from ugliness to beauty. We must become candidates for God's blessing, begin to incarnate His beauty in our relationships, and open these relationships to the non-Christian. Once the "music" has been heard, expect to be asked for the "reason for the hope (beauty) that you have."

Play the music, and they'll be candidates for the Word! Sheldon Vanauken says it so well! "The best argument for Christianity is Christians; their joy, their certainty, their completeness. But the strongest argument against Christianity is also Christians —when they are sombre and joyless, when they are self-righteous and smug in complacent consecration, when they are narrow and repressive, then Christianity dies a thousand deaths."[3]

When the joy, the certainty, the completeness, and the beauty of a Christian community is cultivated and communicated, evangelism is the glorious result. I have written this book with the intention of nudging the church toward its divine birthright so that it will explode its beauty into Jerusalem, Judea, Samaria, and the uttermost parts of your world.

Introduction, Notes

1. James Engel, *Contemporary Christian Communications* (Nashville: Thomas Nelson, Inc., 1979), p. 27.
2. C. S. Lovett, *Witnessing Made Easy* (Baldwin Park, CA: Personal Christianity, 1979), p. 20.
3. Sheldon Vanauken, *A Severe Mercy* (New York: Harper and Row, 1977), p. 85.

Part 1

Evangelism As It Should Be

Chapter 1

Embarking On a Pilgrimage to Beauty

What do Cinderella, princesses kissing frogs, and ugly ducklings have in common? All three describe a pilgrimage to beauty. Why does the delightful story of Cinderella endear itself to the hearts of millions of people around the world? Because one persistent prince is able to transform a lowly, unkempt, awkward servant girl into a charming, beautiful, graceful princess. Whether it be princesses kissing frogs, ugly ducklings becoming swans, or abused Cinderellas becoming belles of the ball, beauty is always irresistible. Its secrets are priceless, its presence is magnetic. It should come as no surprise, then, that God's strategy for evangelism involves a beautiful bride.

A beautiful bride—that's the key to evangelism. Brides bypass intellects and capture hearts. Tough, calloused, hardened men are known to weep in their presence. Men of steel melt and their wives get misty-eyed. Ideally, a bride is the epitome of all that is right and beautiful. She's a symbol of purity, hope, purpose, trust, love, beauty, and wholeness in a world pockmarked with ugliness. The bride motif, found in both testaments, is used by God to illustrate His strategy for attracting mankind to the availability of His life-changing grace.

The name of God's bride in the Old Testament is Israel. In the

New Testament it is the church. Both Israel and the church are described as brides whose beauty is traced to God's love for them. Our focus for the moment is the church. Paul tells us that Christ loved the church and gave himself for her to "present her to himself as a radiant church, without stain or wrinkle or any other blemish, but holy and blameless" (Ephesians 5:27). This verse about Christ's love for the church has great bearing upon God's evangelism strategy.

THE CALLING FORTH OF BEAUTY

Carefully take note of the *purpose,* the *product,* and the *process* of Christ's love. The purpose of Christ's love is to call forth beauty (without stain or wrinkle). The product of Christ's love is said to be "holiness and blamelessness." "Holy" describes the *character* of the church; "blameless" describes her *conduct.* Christ's love of His bride is the *process* by which He develops her holy character and blameless conduct.

As a successful agent for change, there is nothing comparable to love. Its transforming power is beautifully real—and miraculously effective. Years ago a stray dog adopted the nine Aldrich children. Obviously mistreated and suffering from malnutrition, the dog's reactions made it clear love was not part of its daily experience. With its tail between its legs, it would slink around, cowering as though it expected to be struck, abused, or driven away. We named the dog Tex and started loving our newest family member as only kids can do. We weren't psychologists, nor did we know of love's power to change. We just liked animals. But love won out and Tex was transformed into a different dog. Eager to join our every antic, quick to trust our leadership in each situation, and overflowing with love that came in the form of licks and enthusiastic nuzzles, Tex literally became a new creature when love became a part of his experience. We, too, can be transformed by this process. Broken by sin and blemished by infinite imperfections, we have not been excluded from Christ's love.

Love involves nourishing and cherishing. The word nourish is a behavioral term describing the *actions* of His love. To nourish means to provide all that is necessary for growth. Love involves action, and loving actions encourage and produce growth. Cherish describes Christ's *attitude* toward the objects of His love. Isn't it incredible to think that He cherished us? That He goes the extra mile for us? That He considers us of great value and worth to Him? As objects of His love we grow and become beautiful; that is, holy and blameless.

WHAT IS HOLINESS?

Holiness is primarily a statement about the moral condition of a person. But it does have visible, observable dimensions. One synonym for holiness is *wholeness*. We all appreciate wholesome, balanced people. The term portrays one who is functioning according to divine intention, one who is fulfilling his intended purpose and is being restored to that purpose. A man who *is* holy will be growing in his ability to *act* and *function* as a whole, integrated, balanced person. Such growth is an observable miracle because no man can reverse the progressive disintegration, separation, and isolation which sin produces. Genuine holiness is not a static quality. Translated into life and action, it manifests itself through such qualities as integrity, justice, righteousness, and freedom from guilt. In summary, a truly "holy" person is a *wholesome* person.

Holiness is the basis or foundation of blamelessness. One cannot be both blameless and unholy. When we say a person is blameless, we usually mean that, in a particular set of circumstances, his behavior is beyond repute. No one can point an accusing finger at him. His holy character (his basic essence) expresses itself through his blameless conduct. It is also a relational term in that it *presupposes* interaction and relationship with people, events, and circumstances. An elder is required to have the quality of "blamelessness" (Titus 1:7). The term suggests the possibility (and the necessity) of living life to the fullest, and yet not compromising the boundary conditions of God's character. Positionally, the believer stands blameless before God because of Christ's substitutionary death. Practically, blamelessness is a verdict reached by those who observe a life and compare it to a standard.

Such a person or group has credibility, the first essential for effective evangelism. We must *be* good news before we share it.

When an individual, a family, or a corporate body of believers are moving together toward wholeness (holiness), a credible life style emerges (blamelessness), and their potential for effective witness (beauty) increases dramatically. *Because this is true, evangelism is a way of living beautifully and opening one's web of relationship to include the nonbeliever. A person is exposed to both the music and the words of the gospel.* God begins the process and we become the whole and wholesome product. All for the purpose of displaying His Beauty.

GOD'S CATALYST OF LOVE

God's love is the catalyst which makes a pilgrimage toward holiness and blamelessness a human possibility. The theme of Israel as God's bride is useful here. The prophet Ezekiel graphically describes God's efforts to make Israel beautiful (Chapter 16). He reminds Israel that God rescued her from the rubbish heap where she had been abandoned and left to die. The rescued infant grew under God's nurture and care and came to be "old enough for love." God entered into a covenant with her, and she became His bride. As the object of His love, God lavishly poured out His wealth and resources upon her and she became beautiful. (He nourished and cherished her.) Thus adorned, God stated that she "became very beautiful and rose to be a queen" (Ezekiel 16:13). From the rubbish heap to royalty! The familiar words "Do I love you because you are beautiful, or are you beautiful because I love you?" are freighted with significance. Yes, we become beautiful as God loves us.

What an incredible journey. It's the good news journey offered to every man and woman, every boy and girl. It's the gospel in a nutshell. God is in the business of transforming rubbish-heap rejects into royalty through the mystery of the new birth.

With royalty came *recognition*. God put Israel on display. "And your fame spread among the nations on account of your beauty, because the splendor I had given you made your beauty perfect . . ." (Ezekiel 16:14). What did the world see when Israel's beauty was on display? The splendor of God Himself. How was it seen? It was displayed through Israel's culture and institutions. Her courts of law revealed the justice and holiness of God. Her artistic expressions (the glorious tabernacle and temple, etc.) revealed the order, symmetry, and beauty of God. Israel's sociological patterns of marriage and family, her care for the infants and the aged pointed to her God. Israel's relationships to other nations pointed to the covenant-keeping nature of God (as well as His hatred of unrighteousness). Israel's law with its exalted views of personal value and dignity was part of His reflected beauty. Israel's code of business ethics as recorded in her laws was another facet of God's splendor at work in human affairs. In a nutshell, Israel's beauty was the beauty of a redeemed people living, acting, and relating in concert with divine will. Evangelism practices the art of influencing the unsaved in accord with the aesthetic sense with which God has endowed His creatures. They respond to beauty!

Look at that remarkable statement again: "The splendor I had given you made your beauty perfect." *Beauty is the possession and expression of the nature of God.* Faith in Christ makes me a partaker of God's nature. God Himself comes to indwell me and manifest His life and love through me. Through the new birth, I have a great "treasure" (indwelling Holy Spirit) in an earthen vessel (me). I'm a clay pot indwelt by the Almighty God who loves me!

Evangelism is expressing what I possess in Christ and *explaining* how I came to possess it. In the truest sense, evangelism is displaying the universals of God's character—His love, His righteousness, His justice, and His faithfulness—through the particulars of my everyday life. Therefore evangelism is not a "special" activity to be undertaken at a prescribed time. It is the constant and spontaneous outflow of our individual and corporate experience of Christ. Even more specifically, evangelism is what Christ does *through* the activity of His children as they are involved in (1) proclamation, (2) fellowship, and (3) service.

SPREADING THE BEAUTY AROUND

God does not intend for His message of beauty to stagnate. After catalyzing the process of beauty in an individual and a group with His love, He casts forth His people as seed—seed that will grow into a beautiful message. The first two parables of Matthew 13 teach us that God sows two kinds of seed: *a blessed message and a beautiful man*. In the first parable the seed sown is primarily a verbal message, the gospel of the kingdom. The focus of this parable is upon the receptivity of the soil (the target audience) and the factors which influence receptivity. Forces are described which thwart the evangelistic enterprise. Satan works to remove truth. The pressures and afflictions of life and materialistic priorities resist the potential fruitfulness of the gospel. All of us have experienced these struggles in our personal pilgrimages.

But some do respond to the message, and through faith in Christ come to *possess* the nature of God. As they grow (as edification takes place), they begin to *express* what they possess. The nature of God becomes operational and observable in the practical, everyday events of their lives. What a joy it is to see a new creature in Christ begin to change, to grow, to move toward wholeness. As the Spirit schedules surgery, masks come off, bad habits begin to disappear, attitudes change, and relationships begin to improve. These who respond to the seed (verbal message) of the first parable *become* the seed (the message) in the second parable.

The "good seed" of the second parable are called "the sons of the kingdom" (Matthew 13:38). Jesus Christ is the One who sows the good seed and His field is the world. (It is interesting to note that Satan follows the same strategy.) The qualifying adjective "good" indicates that God's strategy is not simply to sow in a specific geographical area a mouth that moves on cue. The word translated "good" is one of the Greeks' favorite terms for beauty. Beautiful seeds *are produced* as they respond to the gospel and *become productive* as they are sown by Christ to reveal His beauty as He did His Father's.

You are God's seed, friend. God wants to take a radical idea (His whole plan of redemption), clothe it with flesh and blood, and turn it loose in the world of men. What a privilege—yet what an opportunity! *You*—put on display, cast as good seed into this world's field, and set as a shining lamp in a world of blackness.

CHRIST'S PERSONAL PROGRAM OF BEAUTIFICATION

God's Son blazed a trail for us during His pilgrimage through this earth's perpetual darkness. He was the Word, God's message in human flesh. His actions were observed and His words were heard. The call of God upon us is a call to share His mission in the world. "First, He sent His Son. Then He sent His Spirit. Now He sends His church, that is, us. He sends us out by His Spirit into His world to announce His Son's salvation—He worked through His Son to achieve it; He works through us to make it known."[1] Besides bringing redemption, Christ came to make visible, to reveal, and to communicate the heart, the essence, the being of the invisible God. His strategy is instructive for us because His mission was the prototype of ours: "As you sent me into the world, I have sent them into the world" (John 17:18; cf. 20:21).

Christ's model helps us see that effective evangelism involves the *visualization* and *verbalization* of truth. Christ's personal communication strategy was incarnational. To incarnate means to become flesh. "The Word became flesh and lived for a while among us. We have seen his glory, the glory of the one and only Son, who came from the Father, full of grace and truth" (John 1:14). In this verse, we have a model for evangelism. It declares Christ's *purpose:* to glorify His Father. It sets forth His *strategy:* to incarnate the truth (to become flesh). And it describes His *methodology:* to be full of grace and truth.

The Word became flesh. Jesus Christ became the visible expression of the invisible God. This was His strategy. He told His disciples, "Anyone who has seen me has seen the Father" (John 14:9). He was, as it were, a "visual aid" to reveal the nature of His Father. He didn't just talk about love; He loved and the sinners considered Him their friend. He didn't just preach on forgiveness; He forgave. And sinful, guilt-ridden people fell at His feet, forgiven and cleansed. He didn't just proclaim the necessity of justice and righteousness; He attacked the unrighteous institutions of His day. He didn't start a Bible institute and establish a chair of theology in His Father's name; He invited men to live with Him twenty-four hours a day. His strategy was to become flesh and live among them.

The term "live among" could be translated, "to pitch a tent." It is used in the Greek translation of the Old Testament to describe the tabernacle where God's presence "lived among" them. The tabernacle was the "shrine of God's glory." Like the Old Testament tabernacle, Jesus became the shrine of His Father's glory. (Is there any "glory beheld" if there is no "pitching among"?)

How again did the Father send Him? Essentially He became one of us. "The Word became flesh. God did not send a telegram or shower evangelistic Bible study books from heaven or drop a million bumper stickers from the sky saying, 'Smile, Jesus loves you.' He sent a man, His Son, to communicate the message. His strategy has not changed. He still sends men and women—before He sends tracts and techniques—to change the world. You may think His strategy is risky—but that is God's problem, not yours."[2]

In John 9:5, Christ declares that while He is in the world, He is the light of the world. The evening before His death, He told His disciples, "You are going to have the light just a little while longer" (John 12:35). With His ascension, the "light of the world" left. But His purposes march on! Ephesians 5:8 says, ". . . but now you are light in the Lord. Live as children of light." As children of light (1 Thessalonians 5:5), we are not to hide our lights (the beauty of what we possess) under a bushel! Christ now plants His good seed as lights so that they can "bring salvation to the ends of the earth" (Acts 13:47). In a very real sense Christ has no feet but our feet, He has no tongue but our tongue.

Full of grace and truth. John helps us understand *what* people observed (the glory) by saying that Jesus was full of *grace* and *truth*. It does not say He was "full of facts and figures," although He was. Certainly Christ as "truth" has great theological significance. He is and embodies all truth. He is the supreme, ultimate revelation of His Father. Jesus teaches us by His life that it is not only important that we understand and proclaim truth, but that *we ourselves become truth*. It is always easier to study and comprehend the truth than it is to *be* truth.

The biblical terms for truth help us understand what it means to *be* truth. The Greek word for truth is *aletheia*. The basic meaning focuses on that which is open to view, that which is unconcealed and transparent. Certainly part of "being truth" is a commitment to avoid falsehood and deception. An Old Testament passage illustrates this part of being truth. In Psalm 15:1-2 David writes "LORD, who may dwell in your sanctuary? Who may live on your holy hill?" The answer is instructive. "He whose walk is blameless and who does what is righteous, who speaks the truth from his heart." Being truth involves at least three things: (1) walking blamelessly, (2) doing what is right, and (3) speaking truth from the heart.

Biblical Hebrew adds another facet to the totality of being truth. The Hebrew word for truth is *emeth*. The root verb means to be secure, solid, or firm. The basic meaning is consistency or reliability. Our Lord is "full of truth." As such He is transparent—free of all deception with no intent to cover up or mislead. Likewise, He is totally reliable and can be counted upon to act consistently and blamelessly. The result of this proper blending of *grace* and *truth* is glory, the glory of the Father.

With the coming of Christ the Old Testament era ended. No longer was the sacrificial system necessary. The rent veil was God's declaration that the old dispensation was over. God's presence no longer is linked with inanimate, physical structures like tabernacles or temples. God has moved. But not without leaving a forwarding address. You, dear one, are His home, His place where He has taken up residence. What an incredible thought. . . . My heart is Christ's home—Christ, full of grace and truth, lives here! We err when we call a church auditorium a "sanctuary." God no longer lives in sanctuaries made by men. . . . He lives in you. You are the temple of God. Look at the following diagram.

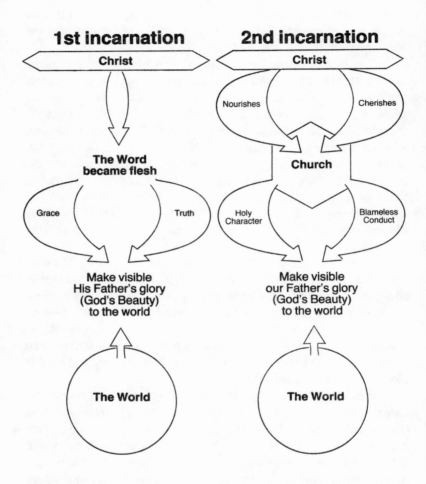

As those who are indwelt by *The* Light of the world grow in grace and truth, they are "being transformed into his likeness with ever-increasing glory . . ." (2 Corinthians 3:18).

Let's review for a moment. Christ's *purpose* was to declare His Father's glory. His *strategy* was to become flesh. His *methodology* was to be "full of grace and truth." He is by nature full of grace and truth. We are not. The effective evangelist must adopt Christ's purpose, accept His strategy, and develop His qualities.

BECOMING BEFORE BROADCASTING

An illustration from the ancient Greek culture underscores the need for a communicator to embody his message. Even the pagan Greeks understood that the "medium is the message." Aristotle focused on three qualities of the successful communicator. First, he must have *ethos,* a term related to our word "ethical." The finest communicator loses his credibility if his integrity is questionable.

The second quality of an effective communicator (according to the Greeks) is *pathos.* This is the root from which we derive the terms "sympathy and empathy." The listener wants to know if the speaker shares his hopes, yearnings, and longings. The Greeks recognized that oratorical skill without a caring heart added up to zero. Paul expressed the same thoughts when he wrote, "I am nothing" (1 Corinthians 13:1,2). Eloquence without love equals zero!

The effective member of the second incarnation must be an ethical, caring person. Floyd McClung said it well. "People don't care how much we know until they know how much we care." Do you care? Aristotle used pathos to refer to a response within the *listener.* I believe the quality of pathos is essential for the speaker as well. Aristotle believed that the listener, having been appealed to by the speaker's ethos and words, is persuaded from his own pathos when emotions within him are aroused in support of the speaker's message. The successful communicator both *has* and *appeals to* the quality called pathos.

Logia is the final quality of the effective communicator. Our term *logos* (word) comes from this word family. The one who communicates *must have something to say.* Ethos and pathos are character qualities and as such are observable. The non-Christian needs a demonstration, a visual aid which reveals that the gospel really is good news, that it really does address itself to the deepest needs and motives of the human heart. This new awareness is music to him, beautiful music! Such an exposure to "incarnate truth" helps prepare him to hear the "words" (the logia) of the gospel. It is my belief that if the beauty of the body is not taken seriously, the cause of world evangelism is ultimately futile.

Unfortunately, most evangelism courses focus on teaching the individual how to *say the words* of the gospel. Not many zero in on *how to play the music*. And verbal *message* of the gospel without the *music* loses much of its impact. The Bible blends both together. For example, Peter says, "Always be prepared to give an answer (words) to everyone who asks you to give the reason for the hope (music) that you have . . ." (1 Peter 3:15).

Peter illustrates the power of the "music" when he encourages wives with spiritually indifferent husbands to shut off the words and play the music (1 Peter 3). The power of a redeemed, changed life is presented by Peter as a strategic means of winning those who are spiritually indifferent. He underscores the magnetic power of beauty by encouraging women to develop inner beauty and use it as a positive force for change.

BEAUTY AS A WAY OF LIFE

Another intriguing thought about a beautiful bride as the displayer of God's splendor is found when we return to the analogy. *God's bride is not a person but people in relationship.* Consequently, the beauty described is one of corporate function and relationship rather than outward form and appearance. This is what our Lord meant when He said, "All men will know that you are my disciples if you meet on Sundays at 11 a.m. and 6 p.m." No, believe it or not, that is not what the text says. They *will* know . . . *if* you love one another.

Christ's bride is the church—people in relationship to one another. God has designed your relationships with other Christians as the primary contest in which His nature surfaces and becomes an observable, tangible phenomenon. Not many nonbelievers are reading the revelation of God's graces revealed in Scripture. Many are reading the revelation of God revealed in your life and relationships. Like it or not, Scripture calls us *living epistles,* read (as a book) by all men. We are literally "Bible translators" for lost people.

Evangelism, then, is stereophonic. God speaks to His creatures through two channels: the written Word, and you, His "living epistle"; His "good seed." What we have been saying up to this point is that God's redemptive love is *declared* in Scripture, *demonstrated* at the Cross, and *displayed* in the body. God has chosen a bride. He desires to love forth its beauty. It is this beauty, the visualization of God's own beautiful and complete character, that communicates to an unhearing world. Christ has proven this method of evangelism; it remains for individuals and the church as a whole to embark upon the pilgrimage of beauty and thus become God's effective communicators of truth.

The factors that contribute to a healthy evangelistic church and usher it along its journey toward beauty will be examined in later chapters. But first one must clear the decks of the misconceptions that have marred the beautiful voyage for many. Such a misconception is the prevention of believers from living life styles that penetrate the nonbelieving community. In addition, once a penetrating life style is acknowledged and understood as evangelistically effective, there must be understanding as to how it can be adopted.

Chapter 1, Notes

1. John Stott, *Our Guilty Silence: The Church, the Gospel, and the World* (Grand Rapids: William B. Eerdmans Publishing Company, 1969), p.15.

2. Rebecca Pippert, *Pizza Parlor Evangelism* (Downers Grove, Ill.: InterVarsity Press, 1976), p.12.

Chapter 2

Avoiding Evil Instead of Its Appearance

"**G**et on the good side of how things work." Not bad advice . . . most of the time. The successful person does find out how things work, and then adjusts accordingly. He does not fight the system . . . unless the system is wrong. Often it is.

Springtime was always a fun time when I was growing up at Aldrich Acres. Animal babies began to arrive, and their enthusiasm and zest for life was contagious. When we let the young calves out of the barn for their first exposure to the world of fresh air, sunshine, blossom-laden trees, and flower-filled pastures, they exploded. I mean they literally went insane. Their enthusiasm knew no bounds. But their world had boundaries called fences . . . electric fences. A wet nose on a hot wire shut down their scheduled frenzy for a moment, until they tried it again . . . ZAP! They didn't have to like the set-up, but they'd better get on the good side of how things work, or the results were entirely predictable and rather shocking.

"Find out how Christianity works and then get on the good side of how it works. Don't fight it." Not bad advice, unless the "good side" is the wrong side. Christ called His followers to a radical life . . . a life which contradicted the expectations and the contrived "boundary conditions" of their religious practices. One of these expectations was to refrain from associating with certain "undesirable" types on the basis of appearance. Although Christ refuted this practice with His own life style, many today would justify and call for this behavior as part of "avoiding the appearance of evil." Is this the right side, particularly when we consider what evangelism is and what going into all the world means?

CULTURAL CONFUSION

Let me reinforce this direction of questioning by listing some commonly held viewpoints within the larger Christian community. Ask yourself the question, Have these viewpoints been adopted because the Bible clearly teaches them or are they simply the views of a cultural Christianity? Many of the practices of Western Christianity are cultural. As such, they may be useful and effective. Unfortunately, however, many cultural patterns are counter-productive and actually work against the evangelistic enterprise—not to mention the truth of the gospel.

For example, in parts of Europe women with pierced ears are never allowed to take part in communion. The Bible nowhere rejects women with pierced ears as unworthy of communion. This religious viewpoint is clearly cultural, not biblical. Should we accept this provincial viewpoint as normative for the church at large, ignore it, or try to change it? What if I live in Europe and my neighbor with pierced ears has just found Christ? What a "joy" it will be to inform her that she is now a member of the church, the body of Christ, but can never participate in a communion service . . . ever. What fun it will be to share Christ with her equally "pierced" friend who has heard she is unacceptable because of something which transpired when she was eight months old!

Note this important, crucial principle: The greatest barriers to successful evangelism are not theological, they are cultural. Many of our culturally determined patterns of life keep people from Jesus Christ! Let's look at the list. You decide whether these commonly held views have a cultural or biblical basis.

Not all of the list will be easy to determine. Likewise you will not agree with many of the statements. Assuming that each statement is embraced by part of the Christian community, you decide whether its support is biblical or cultural.

Biblical	Cultural	
☐	☐	Christians should meet together regularly for instruction and worship.
☐	☐	Christians should meet once a week before noon.
☐	☐	Christians should not be friends with non-Christians.
☐	☐	All Christians should stay out of taverns and bars.
☐	☐	Christians should study their Bibles on a regular basis.
☐	☐	The pastor should run the church. He is the ruling elder.
☐	☐	Wives should stay home, and not work.
☐	☐	A church board should rotate its membership every two or three years.
☐	☐	Majority rule is the pattern for church leadership.
☐	☐	Only elders can serve communion.
☐	☐	Communion should only be served in the church.
☐	☐	The non-Christian is the enemy.
☐	☐	Women should wear hats in church.
☐	☐	A collection plate should be passed each week.
☐	☐	A Sunday school program is a must for the local church.
☐	☐	An invitation to trust Christ should be part of every Sunday's program.
☐	☐	Choir members should wear robes.
☐	☐	The pastoral prayer should be part of the Sunday morning service.
☐	☐	Christians should not smoke.
☐	☐	The elder in a church should not drink too much wine.
☐	☐	Every Christian should be a soul-winner.
☐	☐	Pastors should speak from behind a pulpit.

☐ ☐ Christians should not be involved socially with non-Christians.

☐ ☐ Christians should avoid every appearance of evil.

☐ ☐ An elder should be one who is known for his love of strangers.

☐ ☐ Christians from other cultures who have more than one wife should divorce them all except one.

☐ ☐ Christians should not attend movies.

☐ ☐ What is wrong for one Christian is wrong for all Christians. There is no double standard.

☐ ☐ Legalism is wrong.

☐ ☐ Mature Christians are actively involved in the programs of the church.

☐ ☐ Midweek prayer meetings are a must for the local church.

☐ ☐ Prayer is part of the Christian's life style.

☐ ☐ Ashtrays should not be available in a true Christian's home.

☐ ☐ Wine should never be found in a Christian's home.

☐ ☐ Christians should dress with modest, conservative styles of clothing.

☐ ☐ A mature Christian woman should avoid lipstick and makeup.

I spoke recently at a delightful conference in Switzerland. The local Christian community was upset when the American Christians brought Coca-Cola to the conference. According to them, "Things may go better with Coke," but not if you're a believer. Imagine the confusion of a non-Christian who invited you over for dinner and you refuse to drink his Coke. In the same way, many women who use cosmetics have been rejected because of cultural stigmas relating to wearing makeup. Fortunately, this is not as big a problem as it used to be.

Why do some believers get so upset when other believers drink Coke, wear cosmetics, enjoy bright clothes, watch TV, attend an occasional movie, associate with nonbelievers, and perhaps even have a glass of wine? Please understand, I am not advocating or rejecting any of these practices. I am simply asking a question . . . a question which has a direct relationship to evangelistic effectiveness.

Four Positions on Debatable Issues

The conflicts described grow out of the fact that there are at least four positions Christians assume (or identify with) when a debatable issue arises. On any given issue a Christian operates out of one of four mindsets.

> Professional weaker brother
> Susceptible weaker brother
> Nonparticipating mature brother
> Participating mature brother

Pick a "gray area." Let's use movies to illustrate this difference. The professional weaker brother says no because it is sin for him and therefore sin for everyone. The susceptible weaker brother says no, because he doesn't think he has freedom, and may not know whether it is sin. The nonparticipating mature brother says no either because he does not feel he has the freedom or because he chooses to not exercise his freedom. If he feels he is not free and yet does it, he knows it is sin for him. Yet he recognizes and affirms the freedom of the participating mature brother to involve himself in the particular action or pattern.

	Issue	Evaluation	Conclusion	Possible Danger
1. Professional weaker brother	Movies	It is wrong for everyone	Everyone who participates is guilty of sin	Critical of other Christians who don't agree
2. Susceptible weaker brother	Movies	Probably wrong for him	It is not wrong for every Christian	Participation without full freedom of conscience
3. Nonparticipating mature brother	Movies	Either: 1) Sin for him, therefore he cannot participate 2) Not sin for him, but chooses not to participate	Believes that the same thing can be sin for one believer but not sin for the other	Can believe that the participating believer would be "more spiritual" if he would only limit his liberty
4. Participating mature brother	Movies	Believes he has freedom to participate	It is okay for him, but may be sin for others	1) Succumbing to the "professional" weaker brother 2) Causing the susceptible "weaker brother" to stumble 3) Abusing liberty

As the particular issue changes, so the positions held by individuals change. Probably no Christian is a nonparticipating mature brother on every issue. For parts of the European Christian community, beer is not an issue. Those who have freedom before the Lord on this matter would be participating mature brothers. As far as beer is concerned, I've never touched it. At one time I was probably a professional weaker brother. Now I am a nonparticipating mature brother. Relate this position to the movie-going position. Suppose for the sake of illustration that for a group of people beer is in, but movies are out. If movies are the issue, then believers can become "professional" weaker brothers—those critical of all Christians who go to movies; or they can become nonparticipating mature brothers—those who don't attend but are not critical of those who do. Having seen the positions present within the Christian community, let's develop further some other reasons for conflict.

There are Christians who do not have the freedom before the Lord to engage in activities which other believers enjoy. Paul reminded us of such people (Romans 14). He makes it clear that until freedom to act is gained, they must refrain from certain endeavors even though other believers have complete freedom in the same area. This divergence creates tension.

Many of these brothers are not legalists. They are mature, nonparticipating believers. They accept their personal limitations in some areas, but in no way try to make their pattern of limitations normative for the rest of the Christian community. They do not believe that their more prescribed and limited life style makes them any more spiritual than those with a greater freedom before the Lord. Obeying Paul's careful instructions to them, *they do not judge* the life style of the participating brother. These people, like all true Christians, get upset when there is a misuse and abuse of Christian freedom or when the Christian community refuses to deal with evil and impurity. However, they recognize that the Bible clearly teaches that there is a difference in believers' definitions of personal freedom.

But there is a class of weaker brothers who contribute to the problem because of attitudes which could be termed legalistic. The legalist carefully builds his own pattern of living and then tries to make it normative for the entire Christian community. Spiritual maturity for one who thinks this way is finally achieved when he has closed all the right doors and cut himself off from all "evil." He has to ignore the spirit (the intention of the law) and major on the letter of it. And he makes other believers prisoners of his expectations. His mission in life is to be judge and jury for the rest of the Christian community. He is not "weak" in the biblical sense that his "sensitive conscience" will be injured by the actions of his liberated friends.

It is this "mature" believer who should know better that I call the "professional weaker brother." He uses his misinterpreted "weakness" as a weapon to make the circumstances comply with his viewpoint. From a biblical standpoint he is not "weak" if he is not susceptible. In spite of this, he uses his alleged "weakness" to manipulate others. "Not infrequently it is the weak who is the real tyrant."[1] This form of hypocrisy contributes more toward the death of beauty in a church than any other single factor. A person with this viewpoint needs to be confronted and rebuked with a desire to see him restored to the path of usefulness and blessing (Galatians 6:1).

WHEN PARTICIPATION IS A PROBLEM

Another cause for the upset within the Christian community is the so-called "stronger brother" (participating believer) who is not sensitive in the exercise of his liberty. This person becomes a crusader for liberty and in the process greatly damages the cause of true Christian liberty. Other believers who may be discreet in their use of liberty become footnotes for this person's arguments. These are the ones who may hinder and harm the genuine weaker brother. They also need to be confronted and rebuked with a view to their restoration to usefulness and blessing. The mature believer acknowledges his legitimate liberties in Christ and then limits them when it is the appropriate thing to do. Liberty possessed does not have to be practiced. However, it is my opinion that much greater effort has been expended to bind liberty than to liberate those who are truly in bondage.

Maturity for the nonparticipating brother is not necessarily the exercise of liberty. He will not necessarily become more mature if he is able to exercise more freedom. His greatest growth step is probably attitudinal. He is balanced when he accepts and welcomes the participating brother as a legitimate and God-pleasing expression of spiritual maturity. He must banish all thoughts which would consider the stronger brother "more spiritual" if he would only limit his rightful liberty.

Maturity for the participating brother does not necessarily involve the gradual limitation of liberty. If Christian maturity is equated with the life style of the weaker brother and excludes the case of the stronger brother, it is an illegitimate, unbalanced definition. The converse is also true.

WHEN EVIL'S APPEARANCE CAN'T BE AVOIDED

Another reason for the life-style turmoil within the church focuses around the concept of avoiding every appearance of evil. It is true that there are life-style items which must be avoided on the basis of this principle alone, even if there are no specific biblical directives. But it also can be noted that in the majority of uses, this principle is misunderstood and misapplied. Let's make a couple of observations before we develop this concept.

First, *it is impossible to act in such a way that we will be universally understood and accepted.* This is a basic axiom of life. Some people can't get off the fence. They fear rejection. They avoid anything controversial and numb themselves into oblivion. You can only enjoy the safety of sitting on the fence so long. Eventually it no longer matters. Even fence sitters will be misunderstood because motives are seldom discernible. Only God knows the heart, yet man often says he can discern the intention of other people. This he does by imputing motives—usually his own—to another person. To the pure all things are pure, but to the impure, pure things can be judged as impure.

Second, as we move through life, *it is inevitable that we will find ourselves on the wrong side of some man-made fences.* Like it or not, we will find ourselves trapped by cultural expectations in our churches. If we are considered to be on the "wrong side" of the fence, we either conform to those expectations or experience varying degrees of censorship and rejection. In some minds we have failed and are not living a Spirit-controlled life. According to them, we have not "avoided every appearance of evil."

Without making a moral (or emotional) issue of movies, let's suppose a non-moviegoing Christian sees his Christian brother going into a theatre. The non-moviegoing Christian is offended because he believes theatres are evil places and therefore to be avoided. At this point 1 Thessalonians 5:22 is used to confront the moviegoer, the words to "avoid every kind of evil." Is this a legitimate use of Paul's words? Does it mean to never do anything which might look like sin to someone else? Did Christ follow this principle in His life?

In the Thessalonian passage quoted, Paul is talking about prophetic utterances in the previous verses (19-21). "Do not put out the Spirit's fire; do not treat prophecies with contempt. Test *everything*. Hold on to the good. Avoid every kind of evil." What is to be tested? The content (the message) of every prophetic utterance. What is good is to be held on to; what is evil is to be rejected. The passage is *not* saying never do something which looks like sin to another person. Jesus Christ rather frequently offended the leaders of the religious community.

> They could not conscientiously approve the company He kept; He condoned law-breaking (was this not indisputably "sin"?) in allowing His disciples to gather corn on the Sabbath, or to pull an ox out of a ditch. He gained for Himself the reputation of the 'Prince of Evil' (Matthew 10:25, Phillips).[2]

There is no question but that Christ avoided evil of any kind, yet He did not always avoid the "appearance of evil." Jesus clearly rejected the world's sinful structures and self-centered values, but He loved mankind, and in so doing was condemned by religious people. When the issues were nonreligious, Christ made every effort not to offend. He instructed Peter to pay the temple tax so that no one would have any reason for offense. When the gospel of the saving grace of Christ was at stake, when it was distorted by religious legalists, He confronted such distortions head on. He let His disciples eat with ceremonially unwashed hands although He knew it was offensive and divisive. He allowed them to pick and eat grain on the Sabbath even though this appeared evil to the religious community. He frequented "off limits" places, and befriended unclean people. He was condemned for such "radical" behavior.

His concern was to do the thing that pleased His father. If He could at the same time avoid offense, He did. If in being obedient, He at times horrified men of high reputation—indeed, of religious reputation—and appeared to be acting contrary to the law of God, He counted it of no consequence.[3]

Paul, too, vehemently resisted the attempts of the false religious leaders "to spy on the freedom we have in Christ Jesus and to make us slaves." Instead, he makes it clear that he "did not give in to them for a moment, so that the truth of the gospel might remain with you" (Galatians 2:4-5). When the issue of truth and the essence of the gospel were at stake, neither Jesus nor Paul had any hesitation about "the appearance of evil." Their lives and actions became carefully calculated theological statements which created controversy and generated accusations of every kind.

Christ deliberately chose to live a particular way and was accused of gluttony and drunkenness. Paul reprimanded Peter publicly for refusing to behave in a way which would have been offensive to the Jewish community. Peter knew that the gospel was for both the Jew and the Gentile. In spite of this, he refused to eat with the Gentiles for fear his behavior would "appear evil" to the Jews. Paul (rightly so) took him to the woodshed for it. The same Paul who wrote "Do not allow what you consider good to be spoken of as evil" (Romans 14:16) commanded Peter to dine with Gentiles whether the Jews spoke of it as evil or not. It should be noted that it was Jewish *Christians* who were offended!

Yet Paul cautions the believer to be sensitive to the weaker brother and guard against offense. The believer's behavior is not to destroy another believer (Romans 14:15). It is my observation that it is *not* the genuine weaker brother who distorts the gospel by insisting on conformity to the culturally prescribed legalisms of an unbalanced Christian life style. It is the professional weaker brother, the self-appointed, rigid, unwavering, unstumbling, unmoving, immovable, self-righteous individual who often blows the whistle on Christians penetrating the non-Christian community with the gospel. To this man we must, as Paul, "not give in . . . for a moment, so that the gospel may remain . . ." pure and undefiled in its simplicity and beauty. Succumbing to him makes me become bad news, a hypocrite, and a messenger of a distorted and warped gospel.

LIVING IN THE TENSIONS

The fact of the matter is that the perceptive Christian who has evangelistic effectiveness will always live with the tension between community penetration and the weaker brothers of the Christian community, whether genuine or professional.

The combined pressures of the *expectations* of the professional weaker brother and the *immaturity* of the susceptible weaker brother may keep the mature believer from successfully penetrating his non-Christian community. If he knows before the Lord that he has freedom to entertain non-Christians, to socialize with them, to go into their homes, and to eat with them, but he fears the criticism and judgment of the professional weaker brothers, he faces continual tension and frustration. If he chooses to exercise his liberty and actually mix it up with nonbelievers, he will not avoid every "appearance of evil." He will be accused of eating with publicans and sinners, and breaking the established mores of the Christian community. He may even be accused of being a glutton and drunkard.

Sounds vaguely familiar, doesn't it. Wasn't there someone who was accused of the same thing nearly 2,000 years ago? "If Jesus came back today and mingled with gamblers, the skid-row crowd and the cocktail set, a lot of shocked Christians would throw up their hands and say He was too worldly."[4] I guess He *was* guilty of being a friend of sinners.

Again, Christ must be our model. Christ is our great high priest who built a bridge between God and man. The Latin word for priest (pontifex) literally means "bridge builder." We as believer-priests are to also be building bridges as Christ did. He did not reject the caresses of a prostitute; he touched untouchable lepers; he scandalized the religious community by mixing with the riffraff. He was often where the beer cans and poker chips were present.

"We are to go as He went, to penetrate human society, to mix with unbelievers and fraternize with sinners. Does not one of the Church's greatest failures lie here? We have disengaged too much. We have become a withdrawn community. We have become aloof instead of alongside."[5]

As Radical as Christ

Can we be any less radical than Jesus Christ? The more a Christian is like Jesus Christ—*really* like Jesus Christ—the more effective he is in evangelism. Christ said His life style wouldn't fit in old wineskins and therefore the prescribed, Pharisaical, "religious," pious, pokerfaced platform was ruled out. Christ was characterized by a holy worldliness. This is the model for the believer. But it's risky; it's "out with the wolves"; it's dangerous. When sheep are "out with the wolves," they must obey and trust the shepherd. But when they "hang around the barn," who needs the shepherd? The tragedy in Christian circles is the fact that often the greatest wounds come not from the wolves, but from other sheep. We need our Ephesians 6 armor to protect us from each other.

Why is it that we are the only army that shoots its wounded soldiers, as though to get wounded in battle was a sin? The sin is that so few are even *in* the battle. The few who make it to the front lines though the barrage of criticism of their Christian comrades and get wounded are often soundly scolded for going to the front lines in the first place. Clearly, the safest thing is to do nothing. But I know that's not what *you* want to do. Paul's whole point in discussing weaker and stronger brothers is a plea to recognize *how varied and diverse will be the behavior of the men who are equally zealous in their commitment to please God*. In the light of this he gives some instructions in chapter 14 of the book of Romans, beginning with verse 10.

(1) "You, then, why do you judge your brother?"
(2) "Or why do you look down on your brother?"
(3) ". . . each of us will give an account of himself to God."
(4) "Therefore let us stop passing judgment on one another."

(5) "Let us therefore make every effort to do what leads to peace and to mutual edification."

(6) "So whatever you believe about these things keep between yourself and God."

(7) "Therefore do not let anyone judge you by what you eat or drink, or with regard to a religious festival, a New Moon celebration or a Sabbath day" (Colossians 2:16).

AVOID EVIL . . . NOT EVANGELISM

My concluding remarks about a witness and his pattern of life as it relates to his evangelistic effectiveness will take the form of general observations and suggested principles. _First,_ none of us is capable of fully understanding our own motives, much less those of another believer. Let's obey Paul, and quit judging our brother. Such action is sin. God is the only One who sees your heart and knows your desires. He will judge you, not by someone else's standards (the weaker or stronger brother), but by His own. That is both an encouragement (I am not answerable to my brother and his conscience) and a warning (I _am_ answerable to God).

Second, beware of professional weaker brothers and be sensitive to susceptible weaker brothers. Please note that the Christian community has just as much responsibility to _educate_ the susceptible brother as it does to guard against offending him. If a basically nonparticipative pastor fails to affirm the legitimacy of a more participative, penetrating life style, he is guilty of hindering the evangelistic effectiveness of the penetrating life style and perpetuating the susceptibility of the weaker brother.

We make it sound as though the information which the susceptible brother needs to make choices is somehow unavailable. What does he need to know? He needs to know about morally neutral areas. All things are lawful (he has freedom); but not everything edifies or builds. He must learn about matters of conscience. One must not violate his conscience in the area of doubtful things. His conscience establishes his personal boundary conditions. As long as it is bound in a particular area, he is also bound. He must know that an action can be sin for him today (if he violates his conscience), and may not be sin for him a year from now (if he comes to a point of freedom of conscience in this area). He must recognize that freedoms vary with respect to the individual. What is right for one Christian may be wrong for him; therefore, he must not allow the freedom of another to give him an excuse for sin. He must be instructed about use and misuse of freedom. Some believers will misuse their freedom and set a bad example for him. Conversely, some will use their freedom effectively as a bridge to the non-Christian culture. He must know how to use his freedom. His own liberty does not have to be exercised. He may need to limit it under certain circumstances. He must understand that liberty is contextual and situational. What is seen as liberty for one Christian community may be considered either license or sin in another. He cannot be bound by the collective conscience of the Christian world. Whatever he does in his particular geographical context in one way or another will be considered wrong or imprudent somewhere else. Finally, he must know how to exercise his conscience. He must not bind others by his own convictions. He must be taught to recognize and respect other Christians' freedom. It is the duty and responsibility of every pastor or Christian person to educate the susceptible Christian. There is no reason for him to remain in this category for more than a very short time.

Third, we must recognize and affirm the legitimacy of divergent life styles and learn to live with the tensions they create. Paul makes it clear that "meat eaters" and "non-meat eaters" are both legitimate members of the body of Christ. "He who eats meat, eats to the Lord, for he gives thanks to God" (Romans 14:6). Eating meat offered to idols was offensive to some, and totally nonoffensive to others. Some had freedom to eat it, others didn't. As a general rule, meat eaters make better evangelists. We will see why in a later chapter. Unfortunately, many churches have polarized around the non-meat-eating life style and made it normative for all Christians. It has become *the* definition of spirituality. The healthy church affirms both meat eaters and non-meat eaters and encourages them to live together in creative tension.

Fourth, we must not sacrifice truth to gain the approval of men. There was a searching community whose understanding of the gospel would have been distorted had Jesus or Paul succumbed to the pressures of conformity. There is a time when those who refuse communion because of pierced ears must be opposed because it is a distortion of the saving grace of Jesus Christ. There is a time when those who criticize believers who fraternize, associate, befriend, and love non-Christians must be opposed. They violate truth and distort the gospel when they parade their legalisms before others. There is a time when those churches who proclaim truth and produce ugliness must be opposed and rebuked because they mar the bride's beauty and present a caricature of Christ to the world.

Fifth, let's be certain we avoid evil. *Who* we are determines *where* we are. Not all are free to mix with non-Christians . . . but some are. Let's let them do it. If you're made of dynamite, don't stoke blast furnaces. The more mature we are in Christ, the better prepared we are to penetrate deeply and effectively into our non-Christian communities. The mark of true maturity is not withdrawal, it's penetration.

Sixth, as a general rule, the farther a Christian is away from effective personal evangelism the more he is involved in criticism. Many in the church are like caged hunting dogs. With no birds to hunt they spend their time nipping, scrapping, and fighting with each other. Turned loose to fulfill their destiny, to pursue their quarry, to fulfill their "great commission," they automatically stop biting and fighting each other. There are more important things to do. I've tested this out, particularly with pastors. Inevitably the pastor who objects to befriending non-Christians has never befriended one himself.

Seventh, identifying with the world is not the same as being identical with it. As Rebecca Pippert puts it, Christ was effective because of His radical identification and His radical difference. His radical identification with the human race was totally out of character with the religious communities' expectations of God. Yet it was the reality of Christ's humanness that called attention to His deity. It was often in the context of His similarity with mankind that His deity (His radical difference) came bursting through. Holiness and blamelessness make identification a safe enterprise. The disciplines of the Christian life are essential if identification is going to be *redemptive* rather than *destructive*.

Eighth, compromise of some sort is inevitable in life. As life moves on we discover that *some* of our dearly held axioms must succumb to the ax of maturity and truth. As a youngster I was convinced that no one who smoked was a Christian. Today I know better, and view such believers as brothers, although I still question the wisdom of their habit. One cannot live, work, or minister with another without compromise. Unity demands it. The carpet cannot be solid red, blue plaid, or forest green at the same time. Someone has to compromise.

Yet all of us must have absolutes which we will not compromise. These absolutes are rooted solidly (and clearly) upon God's inerrant Word. Admittedly, the very word "compromise" is somewhat odious. In reality it is a necessary term. In youth, white is white, and black is black. Everything is so clear, so seemingly obvious. But age changes things. Age brings a new perspective so that we can see the necessity of compromise.

> When we are young, we refuse to compromise. When we are in our twenties, we see we have to compromise. When we are in our thirties, we are willing to compromise. When we are in our forties, we learn to compromise. Finally, we discover that compromise is what life is all about.[6]

In the words of Elisabeth Elliot, "Let us not be Pharisees in our certainty of what God could or could not permit." A bride is made of many parts, most of which are different in form, function, and purpose. To be beautiful, each part must be allowed to function properly, according to *divine specifications*. Let Christ build His church *and* judge its effectiveness. He as the Author of evangelism is the only Person who can determine motives as well as methods.

When freedom to share with others by stepping across falsely imposed boundaries is recognized, a Christian must be sensitive to the problems and challenges such a step poses. He must be ready to enter another culture—without rejecting it, but without selling out to it, either. If he eats meat, he must not begin to worship the gods of the meat eaters. The next chapter tells how.

Chapter 2, Notes

1. Anders Nygren, *Commentary on Romans* (Philadelphia: Fortress Press, 1975), p. 445.

2. Elisabeth Elliot, "What is Meant by the Appearance of Evil?", *Witness —Winnipeg Bible College* 56 (1978):3.

3. Ibid., p. 5

4. Leighton Ford, *The Christian Persuaders* (New York: Harper & Row, 1966), p. 12.

5. John R. Stott, *Our Guilty Silence: The Church, the Gospel and the World* (Grand Rapids: William B. Eerdmans Publishing Company, 1969), p. 62.

6. Edward Dayton, "Compromise," *MARC Newsletter,* September 1978, p. 3.

Chapter 3

Eating Meat and Evangelizing

*C*ome with me on an imaginary journey into the home of a non-Christian neighbor. We are invisible. In the den, a *Playboy* magazine tops the stack of reading material on the coffee table causing a yellow caution light to flash on our spiritual dashboard. In the corner opposite a mute TV set sprawls the man of the house, feet propped up, beer can clenched in his fist. The yellow light flashes again. Bob's tired from a rough day in the dog-eat-dog world. His mind is reliving the events of another day's scramble for the almighty dollar. A day of cutting corners, pressure, compromise, and more pressure. He's not entirely happy with what the realities of the marketplace have done to his boyhood ideals. But then, doesn't everyone have a price? He smiles when he thinks of his new Mercedes. Couldn't really afford it, but nobody needs to know. Besides, if he can close the Smith deal quickly, he'll make a killing. Isn't that what life's all about?

The driving beat of a rock record with its screaming vocalist has his sing-along-daughter's undivided attention. The caution light flashes again. Glancing at his bookshelf, it's obvious that some of Bob's books did not come from the local library. Marian, the librarian, would have surely blushed. We don't blush—invisible people can't—but our yellow light continues to flash. Mom

(Pam) puts down her cigarette long enough to answer the phone. She explains to the caller that they won't make the bridge party. They're going to a movie with some unexpected guests. The yellow light is at it again.

Sally, the teen-age daughter, finally shuts the music off and disappears. She's got a date with her steady. They're going to the disco. She's on the pill. Yellow lights flash. Jim, Bob's son from a previous marriage, bursts into the den demanding his overdue allowance. His timing is poor. Bob shares with him a piece of his mind he can ill afford to lose. His comments about Jim's shoulder length hair add fuel to the fire. There are hard words. The air turns blue. Again, our spiritual dashboards light up. No grace is offered before the meal and there is little grace expressed during it.

But things calm down. Jim retires to his room. The rock star posters (not to mention the eastern guru's grinning portrait) do a number on our spiritual dashboards. The books on transcendental meditation don't help. It's a good thing we don't see the drugs stashed away under his mattress.

Responding to the doorbell, Bob welcomes Karen and Ned, friends from way back. Bob pours them drinks as they make small talk together. Karen and Pam disappear for a few minutes, providing Bob and Ned an opportunity to exchange some off-color stories salted with four letter words. Their boisterous laughter almost drowns out Karen and Pam's discussion of you, their next door neighbor.

They can't seem to figure you out. You seem to enjoy going to your church and sitting while someone preaches at you. They shake their heads at the thought. It must be a terrible waste. And you wouldn't let your kids go to the ball game on Sunday even though they really wanted to go. This they can't understand. Pam shares how they had offered to take your teen-age son to the school dance, but you explained that you didn't allow your children to dance. That was okay, but your comments about being born again and accepting Christ and submitting to husbands didn't communicate. It is almost as though you had your own language. Your more spartan, conservative life style doesn't go unnoticed either. It makes Pam feel somewhat guilty about her love of flamboyant, expensive styles. But what is wrong with looking good, eating good, and living good while it all lasts. You can't take it with you. It must be a difference in values.

They consider your submission ideas to be a cop out. Your husband is viewed as a chauvinist, although he seems to be a nice guy. This "chain of command" stuff has to go.

Pam says she feels you are in the dark ages intellectually. How can anyone believe that stuff about a virgin birth, miracles, and angels? Why would anyone involve himself with such an outdated life style?

Pam knows you are better than she and admits she probably needs religion. In fact, she feels uncomfortable around you. They laugh together as she describes herself as your "project" in spite of her Christian Science background.

Earrings finally in place, lipstick properly applied, they rejoin their husbands and drive off to laugh through an R-rated movie. Isn't this the good life?

CULTURE, CONVERSION, CONFLICTS

Why the yellow lights? Why the feelings of awkwardness and inadequacy? Because Christians are members of a new order, a new family with a redeemed set of beliefs, values, customs, and institutions. In Christ we are new creations and become members of a new culture. We are citizens of heaven. We are aliens, strangers, and pilgrims on this earth. It is not our home. We are different—radically different. Conversion has brought a radical change of allegiance. The new birth forces us to rethink our most foundational convictions. Our values, our entire world view, and our belief structure change.

We call the beliefs, values, customs, and characteristics of a particular group its culture. In a nutshell, culture is a body of ready-made solutions to the challenges, tensions, and problems of life. It is our emotional home, our mental furniture, an acquired way of coping. At the center of a culture is an understanding of the universe and man's place in it. This important world view may be theistic or atheistic. From it are established standards of behavior, values, and conduct. Within any given culture, there are numerous subcultures. For example, research indicates that within the sub-culture of the world of hobos there are at least fifty distinct types, each with its own language, attitudes, and customs. As mentioned earlier, conversion involves "a transfer from one community to another, that is, from fallen humanity to God's new humanity."[1]

The experience of being a "new creature" in Christ often causes great conflict. It is not unusual for a new Christian to reject everything associated with the past. Often he withdraws complete-ly from his social environment, abandoning all previous webs of relationships. The radical nature of conversion makes it inevitable that it will strike at the root of the new convert's cultural heritage.

RESPONDING TO CULTURE

As the new believer grows in grace, his world view, his fun-damental convictions, his values, his beliefs, and his social pat-terns must come under the lordship of Christ. All fundamental con-victions must be reexamined. The Christian's response to culture is important because an understanding of culture is critical to effec-tive evangelism. Throughout the history of Christianity the church has responded to the relationship between conversion and human culture in at least four ways.[2]

Rejection

The first response to human culture is *rejection*. This life style of withdrawal and isolation is not limited to monastic orders or religious sects. It is not uncommon among Christians in many of our churches.

> This "closed corporation" mentality, a sort of Christian isolationism, has been a constant barrier to evangelism. Many Christians have been so afraid of being contami-nated by worldliness that they have avoided any social contacts with unconverted persons. As a result, they have no natural bridge for evangelism; what witnessing they do is usually artificial and forced rather than the spontaneous outgrowth of genuine friendship.[3]

Such rejectionists develop their own language, values, customs, and social activities. To them social segregation from the non-Christian world is normative. A radical difference must be maintained. The unbeliever is to be avoided at all costs. John Stott calls them "rabbit-hole Christians."

> You know—the kind who pops his head out of the hole, leaves his Christian roommate in the morning, and scurries to class, only to frantically search for a Christian to sit next to (an odd way to approach a mission field). Thus he proceeds from class to class. When dinner time comes, he sits with all the Christians in his dorm at one huge table and thinks, "What a witness!" From there he goes to his all-Christian Bible Study, and he might even catch a prayer meeting where the Christians pray for the nonbelievers on his floor. (But what luck that he was able to live on the floor with seventeen Christians!) Then at night he scurries back to his Christian roommate. Safe! He made it through the day and his only contacts with the world were those mad, brave dashes to and from Christian activities.[4]

An overstatement, perhaps, but not without truth. Because of their emphasis upon *only* a radical difference, they have a message, but no audience.

Immersion.

A second response is *immersion,* the exact opposite of rejection. These Christians, sensing the need for a *radical identification* with human culture (the world), fail to maintain the radical difference so important to the rejectionist. As a result, they become essentially indistinguishable from the world. Their salt loses its saltiness and effective evangelism ceases. They have an audience, but no message. These believers succumb to the world's pressures, allowing it to push them into its mold.

Split Adaptation

A third response of Christianity to culture is *split adaptation*. This view is a blend of the rejection and immersion options. In reality it is a form of spiritual schizophrenia. This person is a citizen of two worlds and attempts to be at home in both of them. Like the rejectionist, he strongly criticizes human culture as being tainted by sin, transient, and without redeeming value. Yet he "adapts" by conforming to the very world he denies. He drifts with the majority opinion and experiences varying degrees of discomfort. The thought of bringing his faith to bear on the social ills and injustices of his culture never crosses his mind. He has so compromised the "radical difference" that it is neither radical nor different any longer. Association with the non-Christian community is usually viewed as necessary compromise. He is in it (of necessity) but not of it.

Critical Participation

The fourth response to culture is *critical participation*. A dual citizen in heaven and earth, this believer knows that God has him involved in a redemptive mission with cultural implications. He does not believe that the new birth should "de-culturalize" a new believer. Believers are to be spiritually distinct from the world's culture, but not socially segregated from it. The critical participator will face problems from the collision of the believing and nonbelieving cultures, however.

Paul faced the problem of conflicting cultural standards in Rome and Corinth. Some in the Christian community refused to buy or eat meat offered to pagan idols, while others felt freedom to buy and eat such meat. Conflict was inevitable.

Paul's answer to the problem was to the point. Both views were right, depending on the individual's conscience before the Lord. For one, eating was sin; for another, it was not sin. But the non-meat eater had to remember that there was nothing inherently wrong with the meat because it had been offered to nonexistent deities. The conscience-stricken, non-meat eater's response was correct in that he should not violate his conscience. And the meat eater had to be cautious, not because his actions were wrong, but because of the possibility of creating confusion on the part of the weaker brother.

All Christians are both meat eaters and non-meat eaters, depending on the issue. Radical identification demands that in some amoral, neutral areas, we need to be meat eaters. Our Lord was, Paul certainly was, and we should be as we follow their example.

The critical participator lives with the perpetual tension between Christian faith and human culture. Although he is not deceived by promises of utopia on earth, he knows that he can be God's instrument to work in and through cultural institutions to mark men for Christ. His life mission is viewed as obedience to God and a loving concern for men and the structures and institutions in which they live and function. Surely our Lord would have us penetrate the world of government, of school, of work, and of the home. Does He not also will us to penetrate those areas of modern life which all too often are lost provinces to the church: the worlds of entertainment, of the intellectual, of the laboring man, of the disenfranchised—the "pockets of poverty"?[5]

A balance between a critical transcendence—radical difference—and a concerned cultural participation—radical identification—must be maintained.[6] If the vertical dimension is neglected, one faces the temptation of becoming a cultural immersionist: a believer whose actions and thoughts are no different than those of a nonbeliever. If the horizontal dimension is neglected, one faces the temptation of becoming a cultural rejectionist: a believer who has no identification with the society in which he lives. The key seems to be maintaining a balance between the believer's radical difference and his radical identification. Our radical difference is holiness (wholeness)—not legalism or externalism. Only holiness makes radical identification a legitimate option for the Christian. At conversion, the new Christian usually moves from cultural immersion towards radical difference. To become effective in evangelism he must move back towards his old culture, not to reimmerse himself, but to become *radically* (and redemptively) identified with it (unsaved people). Although our Lord expects *communication* without *contamination*, we cannot communicate effectively without *contact* (identification). The following diagram shows the seesaw setup on which the Christian teeter-totters.

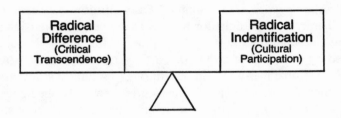

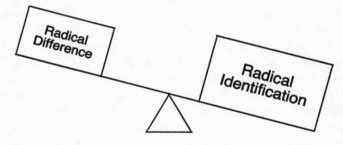

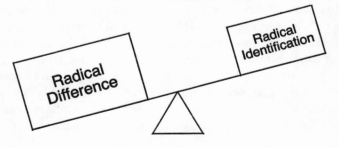

There are dangers involved in trying to radically identify with our culture, however. The Christian who is highly involved with nonbelievers but minimally involved with Christian fellowship may be in jeopardy. He has lots of identification but is in danger of neglecting those things which maintain a *healthy* radical difference. And he is in danger of being absorbed into a nonbelieving culture, thus nullifying his distinctive message.

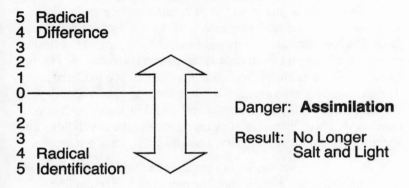

```
5  Radical
4  Difference
3
2
1
0 ――――――――――――――――
1                          Danger:  Assimilation
2
3                          Result:  No Longer
4  Radical                          Salt and Light
5  Identification
```

On the other hand, the Christian who maintains a radical difference without a growing radical identification is likewise nullifying his distinctive message. This is because he is being absorbed into a culture that does not exist outside of the body of Christ. He is so radically different from nonbelievers that no one except believers can identify with him.

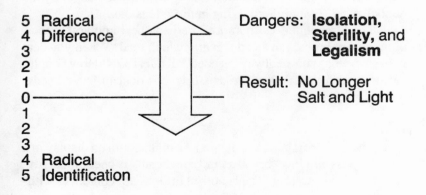

```
5  Radical                  Dangers:  Isolation,
4  Difference                         Sterility, and
3                                     Legalism
2
1                          Result:  No Longer
0 ――――――――――――――――                   Salt and Light
1
2
3
4  Radical
5  Identification
```

DEALING IN THE BASICS

Let's pick up on a principle stated earlier. The greatest barriers to evangelism are not theological, they are social or cultural. Your neighbors, Bob and Pam, probably don't have a theological ax to grind with you. They just think you're sort of weird. They pick up some of the nuances of your "radical difference" and probably read it as rejection. Particularly if there is little or no radical identification. You get sweaty palms and have spiritual hot flashes when you are around them because of cultural differences. Having never experienced the radical change of allegiance to Christ, they don't embrace your values, talk your language, or support your customs and institutions. Consequently, yellow lights flash in your own mind. Those effective in evangelism take the psychology and sociology of a culture seriously, accepting the tension it creates.

> It is only by active, loving engagement with local people, thinking in their thought patterns, understanding their world-view, listening to their questions, and feeling their burdens that the whole believing community
> . . . will be able to respond to their need.[7]

You may be thinking, "Okay; I accept the fact that there will be tensions created by the differences between my culture and the nonbeliever's culture. How, then, do I bridge those cultural differences and become a wanted item (along with my message) by the nonbeliever? (Even if I am living in those tensions.)"

The Greyhound Corporation, perhaps best known for their omnipresent buses, ran an ad recently which read "When you deal in basic needs, you're always needed." RIGHT ON! How simple, yet how profound. When we as Christians deal in basic needs, we're always needed.

Love

The church as a bride is not to be a mannequin on display in a stained-glass window "bridal shop." Her beauty is operational, dynamic, and penetrating. The beautiful bride is not content to withdraw, obsessed with having peace and tranquility. She refuses to sit back and clip coupons on the spiritual investments of her fore-fathers in the faith. Love becomes her trademark, her signature, and her endorsement as she deals in basic needs. It is *Christ's* actual love which is at work through the preaching, fellowshiping, worshiping, and serving of His bride.

Being a Neighbor

Love in Scripture has an interesting contextual bedfellow. It's spelled n-e-i-g-h-b-o-r. Loving your neighbor is part of the greatest commandment! Oh? But who is my neighbor? Nice try. Our Lord's answer to this ancient question makes it clear we cannot determine ahead of time just who our neighbor may be (Luke 10:25-29). Neighbors are to be loved. The Great Commission has not replaced the Great Commandment. A neighbor is someone in need that we can help. He may be beaten up and lying beside the road, but it's more than likely that his wounds are carefully hidden behind a mask of adequacy. Our goal is not to determine who our neighbor is, but to be one. Most of us are neighbors to someone geographically, but few are neighbors to someone spiritually.

So what is a neighbor? The word "neighbor" comes from a root which means "to be near, or close by." Therefore, *to be a neighbor is to develop the capacity to draw near*. "To draw near" presupposes distance. It suggests that there are obstacles to near-ness. For example, the flashing yellow lights are obstacles to draw-ing near. The clash between the Christian and non-Christian sub-cultures is one of the biggest obstacles. Cultural "shock" is very real. Bear in mind that many distinctives of a particular Christian subculture are often just that—cultural, not biblical. In most cases they are a blend of both cultural and biblical beliefs and values.

Let's create a hypothetical illustration to underscore the problems of being a neighbor.

Unbeliever	Believer
• Nonbiblical world view	• Biblical world view
• New morality	• Marital faithfulness
• Materialist	• Not a materialist
• Drinks	• Opposed to drinking
• Ignores Christians	• Views non-Christians as the enemy
• Church peripheral	• Church central to life
• Honesty, integrity are relative	• Honesty, integrity are absolutes
• Swears often	• Never swears
• Made uncomfortable by Christians	• Told not to mix with worldlings
• Accepts culture	• Condemns culture
• Tries to appear perfect	• Tries to appear perfect
• Fears rejection by Christians	• Fears rejections by non-Christians
• Afraid of "conversion"	• Afraid of compromise
• Feels like a project	• Non-Christian a "project"
• Worries about what non-Christians think	• Worries about what Christians will think
• Enjoys dirty stories	• Rejects dirty stories
• Feels awkward	• Feels awkward, doesn't know how to relate
• Doesn't attend Christian events	• Doesn't attend non-Christian events
• Has no understanding of evangelical vocabulary	• Has a distinct evangelical vocabulary
• Kids in secular school	• Has kids in Christian school
• Possibly divorced	• Never divorced
• No biblical knowledge	• Basic biblical knowledge
• Comfortable in his non-Christian subculture	• Comfortable in his Christian subculture

The effective evangelist draws near *in spite of* these obstacles. It is easy to see how false views of separation, professional weaker brothers, lack of social skills, opposition from believers, and just plain disobedience hinder our evangelistic impact. Evangelism that does not flow into the real world (subculture) of the unbeliever can become a raiding party, a foray into enemy territory, followed by a quick retreat back to safety; instead of being a neighbor who loves.

PAUL'S EVANGELISTIC STRATEGY AND CULTURE

Let's examine Paul's evangelistic strategy, particularly as it relates to the various cultures he ministered in and through. In 1 Corinthians 9:22 he writes "I have become all things to all men so that by all possible means I might save some." Note first of all how critical "becoming" is in the task of "saving some." To win the Jew he *became* a Jew. To win those under the law, he *became* like one under the law. To win some, he became all things to all men (vv. 20-23). In fact, he became a slave to *everyone,* to win as many as possible (v. 19).

Becoming All Things

Note carefully that evangelistic effectiveness is directly related to the ability to *become,* the ability to understand and relate to social and cultural differences. To the Jew he became a Jew. To reach them he honored their noble institutions; he regulated his social life. He refused to blast his way through custom and conscience. I am certain he limited his liberty when it was appropriate. He did not appeal to the Gentile out of the Old Testament world view of the Jew. He didn't practice the Mosaic law among them or make it the basis of his preaching. It was totally foreign to their culture and life style. He tempered his brilliance and power when dealing with the weak. He never willingly insulted their beliefs and prejudices.

The issue at stake is not what I need to know, as much as what I need to *become.* The critical question is not, "What *information* do I need to master?" as much as, "What *identity* do I need to assume?" The radical difference we have talked about must be *biblical* if evangelism is to be effective. To be radically different is not to be self-righteous, legalistic, and withdrawn. To be radically different is to be like Christ. This is our identity and the key to a redemptive identification.

Likeness Rather than Difference

Paul's efforts to adapt his life and method to the target audience underscores the fact that every effective decision for Christ must be made within the framework of *their* culture if it is to be genuine. Paul's strategy focused on stressing points of likeness rather than difference. We cannot expect the non-Christian to become a "cultural Christian" before he is a converted Christian. Whatever evangelistic strategy we use, it must fit the environment into which it is directed. Therefore we must understand our non-Christian neighbor and be willing to build bridges to him in spite of some of the great differences of belief and value.

The areas of common interest do not have to be religious. If your neighbor is a fisherman, become a fisherman. If he's in the newspaper business, let him teach you about the newspaper business. I had the joy of influencing a friend to Christ by doing just that. He was an executive with the *Dallas Morning News*. I asked if he would mind giving me a tour of the entire operation. I asked every imaginable question. I was fascinated by all I saw. We spent one whole day together. I took an interest in his world. I became a newspaper man. Shortly thereafter he took an interest in my world, and became a Christian. A day in the oil fields with an oil company president produced the same results. I became an oil man, he became a Christian. With two of my neighbors, I became a tennis player, and they became Christians.

PAUL'S PRINCIPLES OF CULTURAL SENSITIVITY

The same social and cultural latitude that was exemplified in Paul, the same social and cultural flexibility, must be encouraged within the Christian community. The Christian needs to take the risk of "becoming." In becoming culturally sensitive we must underscore some critical principles.

A Flexible Conscience

First, Paul had a flexible conscience when it came to matters without moral significance. To relate redemptively one day to a Jew and the next day to a Gentile demanded such flexibility.

Where cultures clashed, he undoubtedly violated Gentile patterns when he "became a Jew" and vice versa. Paul is a classic example of the fact that there is a legitimate, biblical, situational ethic. The ethical thing to do when eating with a Jew is to respect his dietary restrictions and order food which does not offend. Likewise, when eating with Gentiles, one should not insist on a kosher prepared meal for fear of being hypocritical or offensive to the Jewish community. Remember that your definition of things "without moral significance" will probably be challenged by a genuine weaker brother. Good judgment is the key.

In every situation, though, *a lost man's soul should have precedence over the opinions of some within the body*. This critical principle must be observed by *all* believers. If in becoming an "oil man" to win an oil man a believer finds another believer nit-picking, the oil man's salvation is more important than the believer's pettiness. The goal, of course, is open communication in these matters so that no one begins to impute wrong motives or presuppose wrong desires. If you have a question, ask, don't prejudge. Things often aren't as they appear to be! Again, our goal is to maintain unity within the body, but not at the expense of truth or integrity.

A Sharing of Interests

Second, Paul was able to "draw near" because he made himself flexible to another man's interests, concerns, circumstances, opinions, and backgrounds. He transmigrated himself into their souls and clothed himself with their feelings, burdens, and concerns. He shared, not only the gospel, but his very life because the people became so dear to him (1 Thessalonians 2:8). He moved among people with the compassion of a nursing mother and the concern of an exhorting, encouraging father (1 Thessalonians 2:7,11).

A Server of Men

Third, Paul's whole life was a lesson in self-denial and ser-- vanthood. Visible self-denial activates powerful human instincts, especially when you are the beneficiary of it. And servants become irresistible . . . by divine design. Such self-denial begins in the mind. "Let this mind be in you, which was also in Christ . . ." (Philippians 2:5, KJV). Christ did not consider His equality with God something He had to grasp. Instead, he "made himself nothing, taking the very nature of a servant" (2:7).

Paul wrote, "Though I am free and belong to no man, I make myself a slave to everyone, to win as many as possible" (1 Corinthians 9:19). He did not exercise His right to food and drink (9:4), or to have a wife (9:5), or to receive a salary (9:12-14). In verse 12 he states that he did not use these rights. "On the contrary, we put up with anything rather than hinder the gospel of Christ." Paul's attitude towards life and people was foundational to his success. He willingly put up with anything to reach lost people. His commitment to Christ and His redemptive purposes were unimpeachable. Every ounce of strength was directed to winning the lost by all possible means. To this end he beat his body and made it his slave (1 Corinthians 9:27). He said "no" to its many legitimate wants and desires. He was a slave to everyone to win as many as possible!

A slave functions to meet the needs of another. He becomes whatever is necessary to meet a need. Shoes need shining? He becomes a shoeshine boy. House need painting? He becomes a painter. Sickness? He becomes a nurse. Loneliness? He becomes a companion, a savior at their point of need. A servant is sensitive to areas of tension, frustration, and imbalance, and then relates the gospel to a specific need. He finds that crack in the rim of the soul, that area of need for which the gospel becomes good news. Then he shares it.

EVANGELISM MADE EASY . . . BY CULTURAL SIMILARITY

The easiest person for you and me to reach has three characteristics. He has a similar cultural background. It's generally true that the more shared educationally, ethnically, vocationally, economically, and socially with a nonbeliever, the easier he will be to reach. The easiest person to reach also knows the essentials of the gospel. The seeds of biblical truth have already been planted, perhaps in childhood. Finally, this person has a healthy social relationship with the evangelist—you.

Your neighborhood undoubtedly contains some people with great cultural similarity. After you build social intimacy, you can speak from the platform of cultural similarity and social intimacy and share whatever knowledge is necessary for your neighbor to understand the "words" of the gospel.

Looking back through this chapter, you can recall my saying that everyone has a cultural imprint which must be taken seriously. Paul's example of "becoming" underscores the importance of a flexible life style which adapts to the individual and his cultural imprint. The point of contact between people and the good news is their need, hopes, and fears. But Paul became all things to *all* men so that he could win some. We should, too. We must free ourselves to use our God-given creativity! Not only did Paul have an adaptable life style, he had a flexible methodology. He became all things to all men so that by *all possible means* he could win some.

> Before we criticize what the other man is doing, we ought to remember Moody's classic reply to a critic who disapproved of his methods. "I don't like them too much, myself." he admitted—"what method do you use?" When the critic said that he used none, Moody tartly replied, "Well, I think I like the way I do it better than the way you don't."[8]

JESUS AND JOHN—DIFFERENT LIFE STYLES FOR DIFFERENT CULTURES

The comparison which Jesus makes between Himself and John the Baptist is an important illustration of the need for a diversity of *life style and methodology* (Luke 7). A Christian in a dissimilar setting in this world should be allowed to have freedom of adaptability, even if it exceeds the boundary conditions of another man's conscience (assuming of course it is not a moral issue). Let's look at Jesus' perceptive illustration in Luke 7:33-35.

> "For John the Baptist came neither eating bread nor drinking wine, and you say, 'He has a demon.' The Son of Man came eating and drinking, and you say, 'Here is

a glutton and a drunkard, a friend of tax collectors and "sinners." ' "

The Pharisees refused John's baptism and rejected Christ. The common folks accepted John's baptism and received Christ. Jesus records the accusations of those who rejected John and Himself. He is contrasting John's coming and manner of living with His own. It is obvious they both preached a message of righteousness and both called men to repentance. It is also obvious they were radically different in their life styles, even though both life styles were legitimate and necessary. Of priestly lineage, John had a right to wear their garments and enjoy their rich food and drink. God had other plans for him. An angel described John's life style to his father before he was born (Luke 1:13-15).

> "Your wife Elizabeth will bear you a son, and you are to give him the name John. He will be a joy and delight to you, and many will rejoice because of his birth, for he will be great in the sight of the Lord. He is never to take wine or other fermented drink, and he will be filled with the Holy Spirit even from birth."

Mark's gospel records that "John wore clothing made of camel's hair, with a leather belt around his waist, and he ate locusts and wild honey" (Mark 1:6). Hardly priestly food! It is also clear from the text that whatever John didn't do, Jesus did. "The Son of Man came eating and drinking . . ." (Luke 7:34). In comparing Himself to John, Christ makes a statement of fact about each of them, and then records the false conclusion which the Pharisees had reached having observed the facts.

The accusation concerning John was wrong. He was not demon-possessed; he was filled with the Holy Spirit from birth. The Pharisees saw Jesus under all kinds of circumstances. His life was open to them. They observed him eating and drinking, they saw Him befriend the outcasts of society. He acknowledged that He ate and drank. They knew that. But they never saw Him guilty of gluttony or drunkenness. Christ in no way abused the gifts of His Father. They were right about Him being a friend of sinners, and they considered that to be sin. It wasn't.

So what's the point? Two radically different life styles are contrasted. Both are necessary and both are legitimate. John the Baptist's life style was a theological statement of condemnation upon the religious institutions of the day. His life underscored the radical difference between the righteousness of the Pharisees and God's righteousness. The corrupt, indulgent, gluttonous priesthood lost sheep to a man whose life personified what a true priest of God should be. It was necessary for him to adopt an extreme life style to focus attention and make a point.

Although Christ confronted the Pharisees on occasion, *His* primary target was the common folks, the sinners. His strategy was to identify with them, to love them, and to be a physician to them. He entered into their culture while John withdrew from the priestly culture. John ministered from without as a prophetic voice. Jesus ministered from within as a shepherd and physician. If John the Baptist's life style is the only pattern for the Christian today, surely Jesus would have "out-John-the-Baptisted" John the Baptist. If John drank no wine, Jesus would have drunk no wine, no Pepsi, no Coke, no RC, no Tab, and very little water. If John ate no steaks from the altar, Jesus would have eaten no steaks, no locusts, no honey, no chicken, no eggs, no fruit. But that's not what happened. John came not eating and drinking; but Jesus came eating and drinking. While Jesus mixed it up with unsaved people, John withdrew and became a recluse in the desert. Here's the point: The church which polarizes around either life style to the exclusion of the other is unbalanced. Meat eaters and non-meat eaters must exist together in creative tension.

Both John the Baptist and Christ were evangelists. It seems that John was more proclamational, and Jesus was more personal. Not many Christians have the potential or opportunity to be involved in proclamational evangelism. We all should involve ourselves in personal evangelism. To do so effectively we must penetrate the culture of the non-Christian and become whatever is necessary for the gospel to become good news to our non-Christian friend. We must free each other to do this. Try being like Jesus! Like Him, we must reach people where they are, in their cultural pattern, using their language and meeting their needs. Adopting this life style of evangelism assumes that our presence as well as our preaching goes with our gospel presentation. As we shall see, this life style involves a rethinking of our personal model of evangelism.

Chapter 3, Notes

1. *The Willowbank Report: Report of a Consultation on Gospel and Culture,* The Lausanne Occasional Papers, no. 2 (Wheaton, Ill.: Lausanne Committee for World Evangelization, 1978), p. 20.

2. St. Olaf College Self-Study Committee, *Integration in the Christian Liberal Arts College* (Northfield, Minn.: St. Olaf College Press, 1956), pp. 61-69.

3. Leighton Ford, *The Christian Persuaders* (New York: Harper & Row, 1966), pp. 71-72.

4. Rebecca Pippert, *Pizza Parlor Evangelism* (Downers Grove, Ill.: Inter-Varsity Press, 1976), p. 20.

5. Ford, *The Christian Persuaders,* p. 45.

6. St. Olaf College, *Integration in the Christian Liberal Arts College,* pp. 61-69.

7. *The Willowbank Report,* p. 14.

8. Ford, *The Christian Persuaders,* p. 68.

Chapter 4

Practicing the Presence in Evangelism

*A*n evening at the symphony can be a glorious experience. When you gather together a group of professional musicians, each uniquely gifted in the playing of a particular instrument, and they combine their talents in performing a musical masterpiece, you would be hard pressed to think of a more delightful experience for a music lover.

But I said "can be" because all of the ingredients are also present for a disastrous experience. If the symphony members refuse to play their own instruments, and insist on playing the instruments of others—the violinists demanding to be in the horn section, while those in the woodwind section want to try out their abilities in the percussion department—you will probably witness a less than harmonious recitation of Beethoven. And if each member prefers a different piece and a different composer, then you will undoubtedly listen to a rebellious mixture of discordant squeaks and sounds the likes of which you will never want to hear again.

There is a great need in the Christian community for believers to utilize their individual talents and play music together which is harmonious and sounds forth the beauty of the gospel. When this becomes reality, the Christian symphony provides the background music, the accompaniment, for the individual soloist to play the music in his or her own personal, private world. Evangelism then becomes effective.

Personal evangelism falls into one of three basic categories: (1) proclamational, (2) confrontational/intrusional, and (3) incarnational/relational. All three types are legitimate and used of God. But is it possible that one type of evangelism more effectively utilizes and maximizes the individual talents of each believer and at the same time gathers the music into a more harmonious presentation?

PROCLAMATIONAL EVANGELISM

The early church was planted because of the strong proclamational ministries of the apostles. They preached on street corners, in synagogues, and in marketplaces. Certainly the gospel is a message to be preached. Although the proclamational approach to evangelism will have validity until Jesus comes, it is not a means by which the majority of Christians will reach their own private world. God has gifted a very small percentage of His children to carry out this special task. And we need the Billy Grahams and Luis Palaus of this world and the pastors who also have this gift.

Most evangelistic services which gather nonbelievers in a listening, observing role at a scheduled time and place would fall into this proclamational mode of evangelism. Generally the audience is passive and unknown to the evangelist. The methodology is evangelist-centered and, because of its large scale, basically impersonal. The exposure is brief . . . usually one or two hours. Countless thousands have found Christ through this God-ordained method. Christians can be instrumental in seeing souls reached by bringing people to such services. Many do, and the results are obvious.

CONFRONTATIONAL/INTRUSIONAL EVANGELISM

The *confrontational/intrusional* model is probably the most common one. Generally the "target audience" is a stranger. The limited time factor makes confrontation an immediate concern, and because no prior relationship usually exists, intrusion is necessary before confrontation takes place. Witnessing to a stranger in the next seat on the airplane usually necessitates an intrusion into his present thoughts and activities, and an intrusion (usually without invitation) into the privacy of his personal world of religious feelings. It means he must stop doing whatever he is doing and give his time and attention to a stranger. With the end of the flight approaching at an established time, the evangelist faces the dual challenge of first confronting a person's religious beliefs, and then confronting him with the reality of sin, and his need for the Savior. This he must do as a stranger whose motives, integrity, and character are unknown.

Three things need to be said about this method. First, it is legitimate. Many have found Christ through such an approach. Second, it is limited. I doubt that ten percent of the body of Christ will ever be effective in this type of evangelism. Third, it allows a much higher percentage of the body to meet unbelievers and give a positive witness with a little encouragement and training. Especially if the believer does not feel it is necessary to dump the whole gospel truck upon initial contact. Sensitivity is the key. A good birth involves a healthy pregnancy. Most evangelism training programs focus their training upon a confrontational approach to evangelism. However, it is naive to assume that the majority of people trust Christ as a result of a stranger witnessing to them during a one-time spiritual transaction. The vast majority do *not* become Christians by confrontational, stranger-to-stranger evangelism. Furthermore, many are being kept from making an effective decision because of bad experiences with a zealous but insensitive witness. Much of the problem grows out of some false assumptions about the decision-making process. We will look at that later.

Training in this methodology of presentation is necessary. People do need to know how to say the words of the gospel. But sending these trained people out into strange neighborhoods as an ongoing program for evangelism can be unwise. This is true if there is no concern for the beauty of the corporate fellowship and no serious sending of the Christian into the social webs of relationships in his own private world. Obviously, a church life characterized by introspection and withdrawal has no other option. It is a neighbor-to-no-one spiritually. It has no capacity to "draw near" and in fact forbids it. Like John the Baptist's ministry it says, "You come to me," rather than, "I'm coming to you" . . . as a friend. Evangelism for those living in such an evangelical ghetto is seen as a regular lowering of the drawbridge and a charge out into enemy territory followed by a quick retreat back across the moat.

How much more biblical to have a carefully nurtured church family whose members are released spiritually, emotionally, and physically to be Christ's servants in their own sphere of influence. The Christian loves his neighbor as a person and evangelism becomes a byproduct of his self-giving love . . . and not the reason for it.

> Just buttonholing a stranger, witnessing to him and pressing for a decision will likely do more harm than good. Most responsible people react negatively and often quite violently to this kind of assault. *It shows a fundamental lack of respect for human dignity and personality.* (italics mine)[1]

My greatest concern is not the inherent limitations of this approach as much as what it becomes a substitute for. It's like eating canned peaches all your life and never eating a fresh one. All too often we are putting cut flowers in the hands of people instead of teaching them to grow their own plants. What a joy it has been for my wife Ruthe and me to see many of our own neighbors become good friends and also trust Christ. They are born running and grow quickly because a follow-up matrix has already been established *before* they trust the Lord. We tie neighbor to neighbor in bonds of friendship. They trust the Lord and we all grow together.

> Much of present day evangelism is of the foster parent variety. The spiritual child is brought into the heavenly world by an outsider who then hands him over to a stranger who tries to bring him into a fellowship which is unfamiliar. Thus, at the start, the odds are against successful integration.[2]

Thank God for those dear saints who are out ringing door-bells on Tuesday night. It is not the intent of these comments to discourage them. These comments are directed to the ninety-five percent who are either incapable of such a ministry or feel they have no ministry in evangelism because the only visible model offends their sensitivities toward people. As a general rule, the confrontational approach should be a methodology reserved for the *abnormal* rather than the normal witness experience.

INCARNATIONAL/RELATIONAL EVANGELISM

In a new, unreached mission field, evangelism usually begins with *proclamation,* moves to *persuasion,* and then as decisions are solidified and converts grow, the gospel becomes a *visible presence.* The thesis of *this* book is that a Christian becomes good news as Christ ministers through his serving heart. As his friends hear the music of the gospel (presence) they become predisposed to respond to its words (proclamation) and then hopefully are persuaded to act (persuasion).

Relate these two methods of evangelism to one another. Both are necessary for the gospel to spread worldwide. But once a thriving church is established, the starting point for evangelism increasingly shifts from proclamation (confrontational) to presence (relational). When Christians live in an established community, they may still confront, but they can also relate. To relate is much more natural and less stressful. I also believe it is much more effective in the long run. It should be noted that our goal is not to avoid stress—we're in a battle—but to increase effectiveness. We are looking, not for the "easy way," but for the "effective way."

Peter Wagner likens presence, proclamation, and persuasion to three stories of a house. The decision process could be illustrated this way.[3]

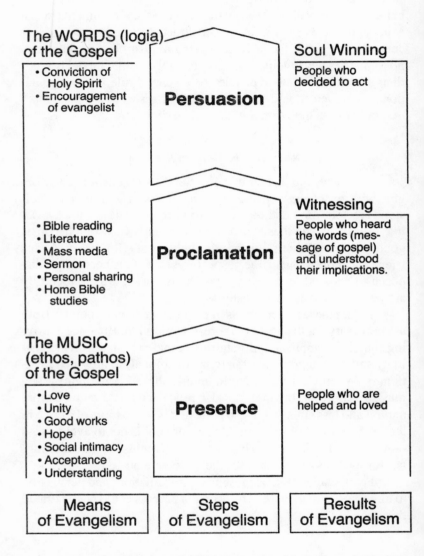

The WORDS (logia) of the Gospel
- Conviction of Holy Spirit
- Encouragement of evangelist

- Bible reading
- Literature
- Mass media
- Sermon
- Personal sharing
- Home Bible studies

The MUSIC (ethos, pathos) of the Gospel
- Love
- Unity
- Good works
- Hope
- Social intimacy
- Acceptance
- Understanding

Persuasion

Proclamation

Presence

Soul Winning
People who decided to act

Witnessing
People who heard the words (message of gospel) and understood their implications.

People who are helped and loved

| Means of Evangelism | Steps of Evangelism | Results of Evangelism |

Persuasion is impossible without some kind of proclamation. Evangelism involves both good works and good words. It should be noted that proclamation as used in this illustration can involve mass evangelism (Luis Palau), literature, mass media, or a personal confrontation. The proclamation dimension of the evangelism process is absolutely essential. How can they believe unless they hear?

But the proclamational dimensions of evangelism seldom take place in a vacuum. A person listens because he's been loved. As stated earlier, people don't care how much we know (our proclamation) until they know how much we care (our presence). Clearly, the second story (proclamation) rests on the first (presence). Presence involves both the corporate image of the church in the community *and* the life of the individual in relationship with the nonbeliever. It is interesting to observe churches filled with new believers even though there is little or no overt emphasis on individual evangelism.

> The key seems to lie in the fact that the body is healthy and growing as intended, without evangelistic frenzy. In such situations, the body itself, collectively rather than individually, is having a distinct evangelistic result. This appears to be far closer to the norm for the church than some of the grand strategies of outreach being practiced today.[4]

When those who possess the nature of God begin to *express* it, presence builds and the stage is set for proclamation and persuasion.

Presence establishes the validity of what is being proclaimed. Presence alone is not enough. No one is good enough to just let his life speak for Christ. Words (proclamation) are necessary to point beyond himself to Christ. Nevertheless, the unbeliever needs to *feel* the impact of the gospel (good news that Christ loves people), and not merely listen to it. When love is *felt* the message is heard. But presence which never leads to proclamation is an extreme to be avoided. We are "fishers of men," sent to catch fish, not frogmen who dive under water and swim with the fish, making our "presence" known. A healthy presence increases the impact of the gospel's proclamation because it helps predispose people to perceiving the gospel as good news.

Confrontational evangelism usually bypasses the first story and begins at the second level. If a person experiences the second story without a healthy first story, he will normally interpret the experience as a confrontation or intrusion. He may make a "decision" (persuasion), but often it is because of either manipulation, fear, or the need to get rid of the evangelist. Having had a stranger as a spiritual midwife, healthy follow-up becomes less likely.

EVANGELISM FOR ALL

As the missionary efforts of the apostles spawned churches, there was a subtle shift in evangelism strategy. Evangelism became more relational as the gifts of the body were "brought on line" for service. A study of the verbs used in Acts and then later in the epistles illustrates this shift of emphasis. The incarnational/relational method simply takes the presence, proclamation, persuasion model seriously.

This is the approach which the majority of Christians can use with great effectiveness. Why? There are at least seven good reasons. *First,* it does not depend upon having lots of biblical knowledge. What you know is not as important as what you are. *Second,* it is truly personal evangelism in that it deals with persons not strangers. *Third,* its effectiveness is directly related to the exercise of *all* the gifts of the body, not simply the gift of evangelism. God can use the gift of helps to win someone to the Lord. Someone's gift of administration might be God's channel of grace for a searching heart. Another may hear the music for the first time through a home-cooked meal made available in time of need. The gift of wisdom can become redemptive as another believer, having won the confidence of a friend, is able to listen and guide him through a particular problem. The gift of hospitality has explosive evangelistic potential . . . if it ever includes non-Christians.

A *fourth* reason why the incarnational/relational method is effective is that it frees the Christian from unnecessary (and often unbiblical) pressure. His primary calling is to witness, to be a light, to play the music. His strategy is low pressure, long range. He is a seed planter who knows when to plant the seeds! He thoroughly trusts God to bring a harvest. This does not mean he is lazy. It simply means he knows you have to plant seed, cultivate it, water it, and wait for the harvest. *Fifth,* the relational model builds the context for meaning. A basic communication premise is that *nothing has meaning without context.* The *content* of the gospel (the words) gains added impact when it is communicated against the backdrop of the *context* of the gospel (the music). *Sixth,* it usually means that at some point in time a person will have to share the words of the gospel. Presence can only take a person a limited distance toward the cross. But if presence is really felt, and is positive, the unbeliever will ask you the reason for your hope! Believe me, it happens.

A final reason for the success of the relational approach is that this method allows you to build the follow-up matrix before nonbelievers come to Christ. By involving yourself socially in various neighborhood events (such as holiday gatherings, block parties, Cub Scouts, Indian guides, etc.), webs of relationships develop. As we will see later, it is out of these relationships that people come to Christ. Having tied some of these people together before anyone trusts Christ, the gospel, once responded to, flows quickly down these established webs of relationships. Friends trust Christ, and are followed up together by a friend. That's New Testament evangelism! This method does *not* exclude the confrontational approach. We do have a responsibility to witness to strangers in a *responsible* manner, a subject that will be taken up at the end of this book.

ESCAPING IRRELEVANCY

Before looking more closely at the differences in using the incarnational/relational and the traditional models of evangelism, we need to pause and underscore a crucial fact with a crucial implication. Our world has changed. It keeps on changing. Sometimes the implications of change escape our notice. One major implication is that our presentation of the gospel must adapt itself to a vastly changed target audience. It is not a question of changing the gospel. It is simply recognizing that the people to whom it is addressed are not the same. The issue is not making the gospel relevant. It is. Sometimes we aren't.

Many forces add to the Christian messenger's growing irrelevance in today's world. Most non-Christians live their lives without a conscious awareness of the Christian faith. Secularization has gradually eroded a Protestant ethic and world view which was passed on from generation to generation. When Dietrich Bonhoeffer wrote that the world had "come of age," he was declaring that man no longer considered God to be a necessary hypothesis to explain man and his world. Today many are totally ignorant of the most basic assumptions of the Christian faith. Another barrier looms large by virtue of the non-Christian's lack of understanding of the most simple Christian terms. Heaven, hell, saved, lost, born again, redeemed, and other such evangelical buzz words used to be pretty well understood by the majority of our culture. That is no longer true. By and large, the basics of the gospel are foreign to it.

Because there has been such an erosion of the gospel's fundamental truths and such widespread misunderstanding of its application, there is not much of a felt need for it today. Also, it is not true that the average unsaved person is desperately searching for answers to life. More often than not, he is generally satisfied with life.

> Some object that people cannot be happy without Christ, but such a viewpoint is naive. Remember that happiness is a relative thing—people are happy *given the light they have*. Furthermore, it will be difficult to convince them to the contrary, because those who are happy and satisfied are a nonresponsive segment with closed fetters.[5]

The rapid pace of life, a shrinking globe, the rise of technology, the more transient patterns of life have created a growing sense of alienation. And the fewer the roots geographically, socially, emotionally, or spiritually, the fewer the needs felt for the gospel. Finally, emotion-tugging appeals are rationalized away as irrelevant. Appeals designed to create a response by playing on guilt are generally not as effective as they may once have been because guilt is explained away. Only a vague doubt lingers. These and many other reasons combine to press upon the Christian messenger the stamp of irrelevancy. This can be avoided if one is willing to change the presentation—not the content—of the gospel.

DEDUCTIVE AND INDUCTIVE EVANGELISM

Traditionally, evangelism courses teach people one basic approach to witnessing. They are trained to announce a blanket gospel message suitable for all. George Hunter calls this approach a deductive model of evangelism.

> It takes many forms, generally emphasizing three stages. (1) The witnesser announces a general gospel to the person with whom he is sharing. (2) The witnesser appeals to this person for an umbrella commitment to the general gospel that has been shared. (3) It is presupposed that if the person accepts this general gospel, he or she will work out the implications of this commitment throughout his or her life.[6]

A vacuum cleaner salesman using a deductive approach would run through the standard company sales pitch even if the lady had no carpets. He would shampoo her floors and vacuum her non-existent drapes. Turned down, he would go to the next home and repeat exactly the same pitch, with a similar disregard for the individual differences (and needs) of his target audience. The opposite of general (deductive) is specific (inductive). The general approach to evangelism is increasingly ineffective in a pluralistic society where there exists such a wide diversity of biblical background and understanding.

The inductive model presupposes knowledge of the individual being addressed. The gospel is then tailor-made to his individual needs. The goal is to discover that point in the individual's life at which the gospel will become good news, and then share it as such. Jesus' method of dealing with people followed this adaptive, inductive model.

To Nicodemus the ruler, he said, "You must be born
again."—he never used "born again," a highly concep-
tual metaphor, in any other recorded instance in the
New Testament. He talked to the woman by the well
about "living water." But when the rich young man
came up and asked what he had to do to have eternal
life, Jesus did not talk to him about living water. Knowing that money was this man's god, he said, "Sell your
possessions and give to the poor, and you will have
treasure in heaven. Then come, follow me." He was basically calling him to a total switch of Gods. On the
other hand, he didn't tell Zacchaeus, the tax collector
who went up in a tree, to give away everything he had.
He simply said, "Zacchaeus . . . I must stay at your
house today." By the end of the day, Zacchaeus had decided on his own to give half of his possessions to the
poor.[7]

Jesus met a person at his point of need. We should, too. If his
need is in the area of marriage, God has good news for him. If he is
struggling with guilt, God has good news for him. Likewise God
has good news for the person who needs love and affection, security or esteem. Obviously a confrontational/intrusional model of
communication will be more general (deductive) because the individual being "evangelized" is virtually a stranger. Unfortunately,
many people have had bad experiences with the generalized, deductive approach and have become virtually immune to it. A caring friend who meets them with the gospel at a point of need is
often the only way they will see through the caricatures to the real
Christ.

The inductive method is a process which begins with the specifics of the individual's life. During the process, the evangelist
finds himself doing at least five things:

(1) *Relating* to the unbeliever's humanness and uniqueness
with a view to helping him solve a problem.
(2) *Discovering* the nonbeliever's problems and needs for
which the gospel will prove to be good news.

(3) *Sharing* how the gospel relates to that particular felt need and ultimately solves his real need.

(4) *Advocating* a commitment which will make the gospel solution operational through the Holy Spirit.

(5) *Supporting* the unbeliever's feelings and thoughts as he moves through the commitment process.

What do I do to win my friend for Christ? I focus on him as a person with a view to relating the good news to a relevant point of need in his life. To do this I enter the process pictured above. At any given point in time I am operating out of one of these postures. The process may involve months of time or a matter of hours. The timetable, however, is not as important as the process itself.

DISCOVERING NEEDS BEFORE SHARING SOLUTIONS

It is important to think like a naturalized citizen of the unbeliever's world. He does things for his reasons, not yours. Extensive research reveals that "people will not listen to the gospel message and respond unless it speaks to *felt needs*."[8] Felt needs are the starting point for communication. From this base the Christian witness moves to sharing Christ as the solution to his real need. Meeting felt needs is often the key which unlocks the opportunity to share Christ. Let me put it another way: Effective evangelism begins where people *are,* not where we would like them to be. As the King's messengers, our challenge is to help others discover how their needs can be satisfied through a relationship with Jesus Christ.

Ultimately, the purpose of evangelism is to help someone solve a problem . . . a critical problem which is literally a matter of life and death. It is common knowledge in the sales world that people do not buy products because they understand the product. Instead, they buy products because they believe a salesman understands them. Therefore, the expert salesman must be a *people expert* as well as a *product expert*. To use the same analogy, many Christians know their "product" (the gospel), but they don't know people. Christians need to think through what the gospel can mean to a searching heart. Besides deliverance from a literal hell, it may put his marriage back together, it may end his overpowering guilt, it may free him from a burdensome habit, it may bring peace, it may bring financial stability, it may solve many of his interpersonal problems, it may be the key to coping with illness, it may be the solution to a tragedy or some great loss, it may be the key to resources for living. Possibly it will be all of the above. That's good news! Every basic human need or motive is matched by some facet of the gospel.

I have used Maslow's Hierarchy of needs for years as a teaching tool. I find it helpful in determining what level of need a person is struggling to satisfy. Motivation to act appears to be directly related to need. If I can link a solution (the gospel) to a felt need, I have created a favorable climate for action. If I'm hungry, I'm motivated to meet that need. My thoughts and desires turn to food. If my need for food is acute, all other needs are subordinated to this need. As long as any need is not satisfied, a problem exists which seeks a solution. Maslow believed that all men have basically the same set of needs and attempt to satisfy them in a definite order of importance—beginning with the bottom of the pyramid and moving upward.

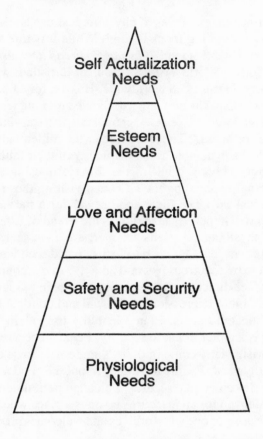

It is Maslow's belief that although all of these needs are intrinsic to the human family, not all of them are on center stage at the same time. What a person says he wants is generally related to his basic need. A person may say he wants a new home, or a vacation to Hawaii. If you ask him why, you will be much closer to discovering what basic need he is trying to satisfy. He may want a Mercedes because he has a deep-seated esteem need. He is unsure of his identity and feels a Mercedes will enhance his image and increase his esteem.

Man's most basic needs are *physiological*. Maslow's hierarchy begins at this level and moves upward. Food, shelter, clothing, and warmth are examples of physiological needs. For a starving man, his consuming focus is food. While it is true that "man does not live by bread alone," *if he has no bread he doesn't live at all*. Thank God for World Vision, a group of Christians who are involved in meeting this need worldwide. Heaven for a hungry man is a place where God sits him down to a table groaning with food. It was Gandhi who said, "Even God cannot talk to a starving man except in terms of bread." Those who enter the millennial kingdom are those who have demonstrated the reality of their faith by feeding the hungry, giving drink to the thirsty, housing strangers, clothing the naked, tending the sick, and visiting those in prison (Matthew 25:34-36). The first "good news" for a starving man is bread which will hopefully lead him to the Bread of Life.

Once physiological needs are met, a person seeks ways to meet his safety needs. Our need to feel safe and secure runs deep. We all want to be free from fear and anxiety. In our country, most of us do not face direct threats to our physical being. Such familiar threats as inflation, depression, and social and political unrest are more sophisticated threats. Man's inability to explain his origin and destiny is another threat to security. Fear can be a reason why we trust Christ. Many come into the Kingdom because of a deep-seated security need. For the insecure person, the good news of the gospel provides an eternal security which tempers all temporal insecurities. Heaven for an insecure person is a place where he rests secure in the arms of one who forgives and welcomes prodigal sons and daughters.

But not everyone has a deeply felt security need. If they are basically secure, their efforts focus "upward" to satisfy their needs for love and affection in meaningful relationships. But sin has blown all our circuit breakers and moved every relationship toward separation and concealment. Yet people have a desperate need to belong. They need a physical and emotional home in which their brokenness is accepted. Does the gospel have any "good news" for the person struggling with a love and affection need? Many come into the Kingdom through this door. The woman taken in adultery prostituted her body to get love and found only humiliation and disillusionment (John 7:53-8:11). The members of her sorority are legion. Jesus' love, understanding, and acceptance were what she needed and longed for. She just didn't know it existed. Many don't.

Every person needs to feel he or she is valuable and important. We all struggle with *esteem needs*. We want others to feel we have contributed something worthwhile to life. We all need affirmation from others. Yet there is no better news than to discover that I am a somebody to God. He knows my name and somehow I'm special to Him. Do you know a non-Christian starved for recognition, who is struggling with this need to feel valuable? Friend, have you got good news for him! Maybe if he feels he is valuable and worthwhile to you, God will use that as a stepping stone to Christ!

When the individual's need for esteem is basically met he mobilizes his time, energy, and resources to become as much as he can be. *Self-actualization* is the need to realize one's inner potential by fully developing his capabilities. The fact that this need for achievement is never fully satisfied is especially frustrating for the non-Christian. Hoping to fill a God-shaped vacuum with personal achievement doesn't work. Thousands of "successful" people suffer from destination sickness. They've arrived . . . empty. They need a worthwhile purpose which links their achievement to something beyond their own self-interests. They need to know that it is possible to achieve and receive eternal dividends. Many would be delighted to discover that there is the possibility of hearing the Lord of the Universe say, "Well done, thou good and faithful servant." Maybe we should tell them.

USING MASLOW'S HIERARCHY IN EVANGELISM

Acknowledging it is but a tool, this diagram of needs does provide some helpful insights for finding needs and relating the gospel to them. The preacher and evangelist can use it as a grid for studying a passage. He should ask himself how the text might meet the needs of people struggling with one of the various needs states. What does it have to say about security, about love and affection, and so on? A sensitivity to these needs can greatly improve his communication (proclamation) especially if he realizes he, too, is working out of a particular need state which may color his interpretation of Scripture. Maslow's model also lets us see how important genuine Christian fellowship can be as it is specifically targeted to meet these needs. Need-centered fellowship stimulates the church to be a healing communion where one can experience security, love, acceptance, esteem, and self-actualization.

The serving dimension of church life can be expanded if these basic human needs are understood and met. Notice how man's needs are opportunities for us to share God's solution as you study the following chart.

Man's Need	**God's Solution**
Self Actualization frustration emptiness uselessness boredom lack of fulfillment	**Self Actualization** satisfaction completeness usefulness purpose fulfillment
Self Esteem guilt failure inadequacy embarrassment lack of recognition	**Self Esteem** forgiveness success achievement confidence recognition
Love/Affection loneliness lack of appreciation rejection isolation dejection	**Love/Affection** companionship appreciation acceptance inclusion intimacy
Safety/Security threatened insecurity anxiety fear	**Safety/Security** safety security peace of mind assurance
Physiological hunger thirst weakness tiredness sickness pain	**Physiological** food drink strength rest health comfort

Preaching · Fellowship · Service

People are more inclined to respond to the gospel when they understand how trusting Christ will satisfy their needs.

George Hunter suggests two further refinements which are full of insight. Relatively speaking, those near the top of the hierarchy of needs are the stronger, more adequate people. Those at the bottom are the weaker, more vulnerable ones.[9]

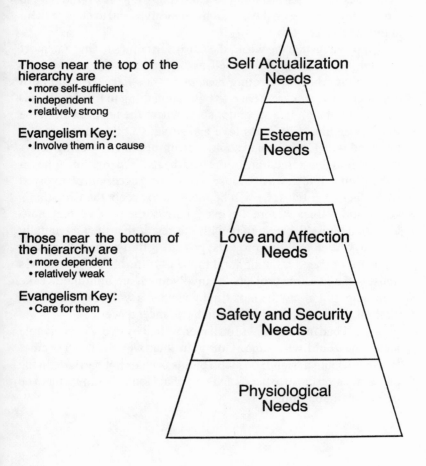

Those near the top of the hierarchy are
• more self-sufficient
• independent
• relatively strong

Evangelism Key:
• Involve them in a cause

Those near the bottom of the hierarchy are
• more dependent
• relatively weak

Evangelism Key:
• Care for them

Self Actualization Needs

Esteem Needs

Love and Affection Needs

Safety and Security Needs

Physiological Needs

Traditionally, the church has ministered more effectively to the "down and outer" than the "up and outer." The person struggling with hunger, safety, security, or belonging needs is most easily reached by being an object of the church's care and love. Generally, evangelism has targeted the love and safety needs and not the higher ones. It should be said at this point that one's position on Maslow's hierarchy of needs is never secure. A stroke, death of a loved one, or an unexpected financial reversal can render a strong man weak in a brief instant. The Christian's job "is to find people where they now are on the hierarchy of motives and to engage them at the appropriate level."[10]

To evangelize the weak, the Christian comes to find and meet a need. To reach the strong, self-assured person, progress comes by involving him in meeting *someone else's need*. We are born crusaders having a great need to have something to live for. Evangelism is not simply a spectator sport where the unsaved sit in the stands watching Christians love and serve. Get the strong person involved with Christians in some type of mission or serving activity. Let him feel something of the heartbeat of redemption as he involves himself in a worthy cause. As he gets successfully involved with other Christians, he will be inclined to accept the Christian's goals and values before he even knows them. I've had non-Christians host Bible studies with the result that they eventually came to Christ. Painting projects, providing transportation, raising funds for the needy, taking food to the ill, refurbishing a widow's house—the possible projects for involvement are unlimited. Take your neighbor along the next time you have a work day . . . especially if he has a special skill which can meet a need.

Paul became all things to all men so that by every conceivable means he could win some. God grant that we will do the same! Begin by being a friend, one who builds bridges not barriers. In the process, camp close to needs and pray that God will allow you to be part of their solution.

Chapter 4, Notes

1. James Jauncey, *Psychology for Successful Evangelism* (Chicago: Moody Press, 1972), p.123.

2. Ibid., p.61.

3. Chart adapted from Peter Wagner, *Frontiers in Missionary Strategy* (Chicago: Moody Press, 1971), p.134.

4. James Engel, *Contemporary Christian Communications* (Nashville: Thomas Nelson, Inc., 1979), p.217.

5. Ibid., p. 126.

6. George Hunter III, *The Contagious Congregation* (Nashville: Abingdon Press, 1979), p.38.

7. Leighton Ford, *Good News Is For Sharing* (Elgin, Ill.: David C. Cook, 1977), p.90.

8. Engel, *Contemporary Christian Communications*, p.117.

9. Hunter, *The Contagious Congregation*, pp.45-47.

10. Ibid., p.46.

Part 2

Evangelism
and the Local Church

Chapter 5

Evangelism and the Church Member

*T*he world listens when Christians love. Consequently, the corporate image of the local church in its community is a critical factor in its evangelistic impact. "In the final analysis, *the church is both message and medium, exemplifying and proclaiming the kingdom of God."[1]* This truth has tremendous implications. "At the very least, it is obvious that the church not exemplifying the kingdom is moribund and ineffective in the cause of world evangelization."[2]

Our world is full of professing Christians who claim to believe the truth, but are producing ugliness. They can't get along. They fight, gossip, and often act like they were weaned on dill pickles. Instead of being an "ambassador in" the world, they are an "embarrassment to" the world. They'll fight for the "truth," but have *no* grace. Truth has not failed. Instead, the edification process has somehow broken down.

THE PLACE OF EDIFICATION IN EVANGELISM

The body of Christ, like a living organism, is subject to disease. If disease goes unchecked, the bride is weakened, and fails to display God's beauty. Israel stopped growing and became a harlot.

Her corporate beauty declined as individuals shifted their loyalties to ungodly priorities and neglected spiritual disciplines. A gradual erosion of faith led to disobedience and sin. Spiritual adultery took its toll. A body of believers cannot remain in neutral very long. It will move either toward holiness or harlotry, towards beauty or prostitution. Persistent, consistent edification is God's antidote to spiritual prostitution.

When the body functions properly, it "edifies" (builds up) itself in love (Ephesians 4:16). To "edify" means to "build up." Edification is the process of bringing the implications of the good news into contact with every facet of life so that it may be "redeemed" (set free for usefulness). It involves a renewal of the mind, bringing into captivity every thought so that it relates to Jesus Christ.

As edification takes place, I become increasingly Christ-like. That is, I begin to *express* what I *possess*. Growth takes place. Attitudes begin to change, relationships are healed, new relational skills develop, negative character traits and habits begin to disappear. And I become a more positive, attractive, Christ-like individual. If evangelism is accurately expressing what I possess in Christ, then *edification* (growth in Christ) is the key to *evangelism*.

Evangelism as a way of living begins with believers who make beauty a way of life. If I am serious about beauty, I must be serious about the church; not only is it the bride (hopefully a beautiful one), but it is also the *beauty parlor*. Built into it by God are all the helps, all the dynamics, and all the resources for change which you and I need to move toward wholeness. The wider our exposure to the giftedness of a properly functioning body, the greater our potential for beauty.

Therefore, we will consider the biblical principles around which a healthy church is built. "'The issue,' says Orlanda Costa, is not 'how many Christians can be enlisted for action or how the church "saturates" society with the gospel, rather it is how we get the dynamic organism to grow internally.'"[3]

There are two very important reasons why anyone developing an evangelism strategy must first look at the health of the body. First, *God is not in the business of putting healthy babies in sick in-*

cubators. Churches in a very real sense must become candidates for God's blessing. The theologically orthodox church at Ephesus was warned by God that if she did not recover her love, He would remove her candlestick (put her out of business). This is the point at which the vast majority of evangelism training courses fail. They focus on training a small minority within the church to "evangelize" and do nothing to bring the majority of the believers into a state of health and beauty. Those converts who the special "task force" win to the Lord often find assimilation into the body very difficult, because "beauty" has not been taken very seriously.

Second, the health of the Body is critical to effective evangelism because *personality is a product of relationships.* That is, we become like the people we associate with. Fortunately, or unfortunately, the evangelist going door to door reflects the values, attitudes, and actions of his peers. When I counseled at a summer youth camp, it was amazing to observe how the campers copied their "heroes." If they thought I "hung the moon," they would soon talk the way I talked, walk the way I walked, and develop similar manners, gestures, and vocabulary. They were becoming "little Joes."

We all are "value vacuum cleaners." Our values are shaped by our associations. This principle works both ways. If we treasure friendship with a person or group, we tend to become more and more alike as we mutually shape and reinforce each other's value systems. On the other hand, if we strongly dislike a person or group we tend to reject their values (whether right or wrong). Thus our values are socially anchored. The choices we make are influenced by these socially anchored values. In Luke 6:40 our Lord reminds us that "everyone who is fully trained will be like his teacher." Notice it doesn't say "he will know what his teacher knows." He will be *like* his teacher—good or bad, negative or positive, beautiful or ugly.

In 1 Thessalonians 1:5 Paul says, "You know how we lived among you for your sake." He calls attention to an *intentional* lifestyle. He is saying, "We chose, we purposed to live a certain way while we were among you." In the next verse Paul says, "You became imitators of us. . . ." He lived *intentionally* because he knew he was their model, and that they would become like him. In like manner, Paul encourages Timothy to "continue in what you have learned and have become convinced of, because you know those from whom you learned it." (2 Timothy 3:14). In verses 10 and 11 he portrays what it was that Timothy knew about him. He writes, "You, however, know all about my teaching, my way of life, my purpose, faith, patience, love, endurance, persecutions, sufferings. . . ." Timothy, like the church at Thessalonica, was an imitator of Paul, who lived intentionally among them.

The result of the Thessalonian believers' imitation of Paul's life style is given in 1 Thessalonians 1:7—"And so you became a model to all the believers in Macedonia and Achaia." Note carefully that the leadership model (Paul's) was imitated (adopted by the followers) and then became the model for the churches of Macedonia and Achaia. Church leaders who are serious about evangelism must see the principle of modeling as crucial to the impact of their local fellowship.

The character of our churches is also cast in the mold of our associations. We are in large measure the products of the people we value and fellowship with. If "God's frozen people" accurately describes a particular local church, visitors and members will ice skate down the aisles *together*. A frigid church neither produces warm people nor attracts nonbelievers. We have already stated that the "belief of truth" is not synonymous with beauty. Many "believe the truth" but produce ugliness. Our actions are determined by our currently dominant attitudes, thoughts, and beliefs. If negative, legalistic, critical, cynical attitudes characterize the corporate church fellowship, then it is quite likely that these attitudes are owned by the individual members whose social life revolves around these people.

THE PRODUCTS OF HEALTH

Lloyd Ogilvie has come up with five key questions which underscore the importance of the corporate fellowship of the church in the evangelistic enterprise. The rest of this chapter will develop the answer to his first question, a question which relates to the health of the body's individual members.

What kind of people does the church want to deploy in the world? What is our product? I am amazed to discover that most pastors and church leaders have given little if any thought to this question. And a mist in the pulpit is a fog in the pew. This truth can be put in more forceful dress. "No one responsible for helping another to grow spiritually can proceed until they have in mind a model of the outcome of their efforts."[4] Imagine a businessman renting a building, purchasing machinery and material, hiring employees, and then turning them loose to produce whatever they desired. No, there has to be a product design; an idea of the intended end result. If believers are to be salt, lights, ambassadors, witnesses, and "living epistles" all rolled into one, what will "epistle readers" be given to read?

What is the biblical profile of a healthy member of the second incarnation? As lights who "make visible" the invisible attributes of God, the fruit of the Spirit is the ultimate mark of a wholesome child of the King.

The Fruit of the Spirit from Galatians 5	
Love	Goodness
Joy	Faithfulness
Peace	Gentleness
Patience	Self-control
Kindness	

A healthy member of the second incarnation glorifies God by revealing the universals of God's character through the particulars of his everyday life. Billboards, tracts, movies, and books are all fine, but not as substitutes for a living epistle who makes love a way of life. Jesus said it . . . "All men will know that you are my disciples if you love one another" (John 13:35). Love bound by holiness is the ultimate expression of God's presence in human experience.

In a nutshell, the product of the church's corporate life and ministry must be a person who has been liberated to love. In 1 Timothy 1:5, Paul tells Timothy that the ultimate aim of his ministry is love. When that love is felt, the message is heard. But sin has blown all our circuit breakers. None of us are lovers by nature. We are basically self-centered and self-seeking. In large measure we are "unbelieving believers." Our lives still contain pockets of hardness, resistance, and unbelief. Although the new birth begins a transformation process which climaxes in the Lord's presence, we all struggle with questionable motives, unwholesome desires, and self-centered action and reactions.

THE PRODUCTS FOR HEALTH

The church, God's beauty parlor, is the transforming community which *should* move the believers toward a life of concern and care for others. I emphasize the word "should" because movement towards love does not take place automatically. Even theologically sound preaching is no guarantee that the listeners are being conformed to Christ's life style of love. It is the author's studied opinion that the dynamics of the local body may have greater influence for change than the Sunday morning sermon. I say this having been a pastor of a large church for seven years. The church described in Acts 2 was a vital, dynamic fellowship of believers that had great impact on its world. Christ loved it and it became beautiful. Locked away in Luke's description of this church are some critical qualities of a healthy, balanced believer. Here the text reveals that the *Holy Spirit uses believers with four distinguishing characteristics to build strong bodies*.

Learning That Lives

First, the believers "devoted themselves to the apostles' teaching" (Acts 2:42). Our church member must be a learning person . . . one who *continues* in the apostles' doctrine. When we cease to learn we cease to live. Many have died at age twenty and will be buried at age sixty-five. The Word is our lamp and light. Scripture records that faith comes by hearing and hearing by the

Word of God. Its truth must be hidden in our hearts (not in our frontal lobes) and practiced in our lives. It has been well stated that to know and not to do is not to know at all. Many pastors perceive the major and central purpose of their church as that of a Bible institute where facts are transmitted from one notebook to another. Doctrine becomes everything, as though understanding doctrine were an end unto itself.

Unfortunately, most people who are exposed to doctrine alone usually sit, soak, and sour. This is true because *impression minus expression leads to spiritual depression*. A diet of doctrine alone will produce soul-sick people who are suffering from spiritual malnutrition. Usually their heads are "full" but their hearts are empty.

> "Far too many people have used the Bible like a medical student uses a cadaver. They examine it, dissect it, perform surgery on it, familiarize themselves with it, and learn its distinctive qualities. But as that future doctor cannot give life to that dead piece of humanity, so these people never get the Word alive in their life. They somehow fail to remember that the people who hated Jesus most were biblical scholars and had Scriptures over their door posts, strapped to their bodies, and quoted chapters of it when their narrow-minded interpretation supported their warped views."[5]

Such churches can become like a baker who eats his own bread while a starving world gazes longingly through the bakery window.

Fellowship That Functions

The second characteristic of the Acts 2 Christian is that he *was involved in fellowship* (koinonia). "They devoted themselves to the apostles' teaching and to the fellowship . . ." (Acts 2:42). This was not "coffee and doughnuts" between services.

While "koinonia" involves the horizontal dimension (people to people), it is not fully understood unless it is linked with the vertical (individual to God). Koinonia involves both the church abiding in the vine for fruitfulness and the body being "joined and knit together" so that it can build up itself in love.

It is the "fellowship of the Spirit" which gives the dynamic, living, healing quality to the "fellowship of the believers." In 2 Corinthians 13:14 Paul prays that "the fellowship of the Holy Spirit" may be with the believers in Corinth (cf. Philippians 2:1). Consequently, genuine fellowship cannot be duplicated outside the church. It is an atmosphere, an environment, a context, and a set of attitudes and actions which grow and develop as Spirit-controlled believers meet and share their lives and giftedness together. It occurs when believers are together *under the direction of the Holy Spirit,* in an atmosphere conducive to the Spirit's empowering the body's gifts to change lives.

The Acts 2 Christian was a fellowshiping person. When he hurt he didn't bite a bullet and ride off into the sunset alone. He learned that the fellowship of believers was his source of strength, encouragement, rebuke, and motivation—the key to his growth. Fellowship takes place when pastoral leaders are faithful stewards of the gifts of the *entire body*. Most churches have one or more "official pastors" . . . and sometimes hundreds of "pastors on ice" who are never encouraged to minister because they lack "proper" training and certification.

The healthy believer grows because he has vital contact with gifts of the *entire* body, not just the pastor on Sunday morning. It is sometimes difficult to recognize and appreciate the fact that although many in a congregation have no formal training, some often know the Lord more intimately than the pastor. Others have valuable personal experiences which the pastor lacks. Some have gifts which the pastor doesn't have and which need to be exercised if the church is to be balanced.

True fellowship and the free exercise of gifts are companions which are inseparable. A church can't have one without the other. All church programs should be evaluated in the light of their contribution to the free flow of the giftedness of the body. If the believer's sole exposure to the body is a one-way, monological communication on Sunday morning, chances are he does not experience the body as a healing communion.

The beauty-building body is always a body in which the believer is free to function properly. When the whole body functions under the Spirit's leadership, the believer is experiencing "fellowship" and the unbeliever sees "beauty." The "one anothers" of the New Testament give us a helpful portrait of the kinds of behavioral actions which characterize the unique, divinely enabled fellowship of believers. Imagine the impact upon nonbelievers who are allowed to observe believers relating to each other in this way. They will ask us the reason for the hope that is in us.

Reference	Statement
Romans 12:10	Be devoted to one another Give preference to one another
Romans 12:16	Be of same mind toward one another
Romans 13:8	Love one another
Romans 14:13	Let us not judge one another
Romans 14:19	Pursue the things that make for the building up of one another
Romans 15:5	Be of the same mind with one another
Romans 15:7	Accept one another
Romans 15:14	Admonish one another
1 Corinthians 12:25	Care for one another
Galatians 5:13	Serve one another
Galatians 6:2	Bear one another's burdens
Ephesians 4:1-2	Show forebearance to one another
Ephesians 4:32	Be kind to one another
Ephesians 5:18-21	Speak to one another in psalms and hymns and spiritual songs Be subject to one another
Colossians 3:9	Lie not to one another
Colossians 3:12-13	Bear with one another Forgive each other
Colossians 3:16	Teach and admonish one another
1 Thessalonians 3:12	Increase and abound in love for one another

1 Thessalonians 4:18	Comfort one another
Hebrews 3:13	Encourage one another
Hebrews 10:23-25	Stimulate one another to love and good works
James 4:11	Do not speak against one another
James 5:9	Do not complain against one another
James 5:16	Confess your sins to one another Pray for one another
1 Peter 1:22	Love one another
1 Peter 4:9	Be hospitable to one another
1 Peter 5:5	Clothe yourselves with humility toward one another
1 Peter 5:14	Greet one another with a kiss of love
1 John 3:11	Love one another
1 John 3:23	Love one another
1 John 4:7	Love one another
1 John 4:11	Love one another
1 John 4:12	Love one another
2 John 5	Love one another

One can visualize Jesus Christ graphically fulfilling the list of "body functions." We are called to do the same! Christ does His work of evangelism, not only through our teaching, but also through our fellowship. Fellowship is the context in which the contagion of the good news is "caught." Its significance for evangelism is not widely perceived. In the early church, however, it probably attracted as many to the Savior as the apostolic preaching. Here we need to observe another important principle. "Effective communication of the gospel begins with a demonstration of its relevance."[6] Incidentally, some of the best fellowship springs from the overflow of successful, consistent evangelism.

What kind of a person do we want to deploy into the world? *Someone who is devoting himself to the apostles' teaching and to the fellowship.*

Worship That Witnesses

Acts 2 goes on to describe our model as one who *worships*. This is the third quality of a balanced believer. "They devoted themselves . . . to the breaking of bread and to prayer . . . praising God" (2:42,47). Worship is *acknowledging the person and presence of God and responding with praise, thanksgiving, and obedience!* What kind of a person is the worshiping Christian? The worshiping Christian is not a worrying Christian. God's presence makes worship an antidote to worry. Surrounded by enemies, one who worships can sit down to a leisurely meal because *God* prepares "a table before me in the presence of my enemies" (Psalm 23:5). The worshiping Christian affirms the presence of God's rod and staff in the midst of enemy territory when the battle rages. Our Acts 2 Christian lived in a bloody, ruthless, cruel age in which his life was continually in danger because of the insane hatred of Christians by the Roman emperors. Martyrdom was common. The ranks of the local fellowship were thinned regularly by Rome's murderers. Yet the church grew, thrived, and worshiped triumphantly, proclaiming in word and deed the Lord's actual, genuine, observable presence among them. The song says it so well, "Have you seen Jesus My Lord? He's here in plain view. . . ." The early church made Him visible, and the results are history.

One of the side benefits of genuine worship is what I call attitude formation and maintenance. The worshiping person is a positive person because he has a certain, solid hope regardless of life's circumstances. He is a victor, a participant in God's sovereign, unalterable purposes. As he grows in his understanding of doctrine his worship deepens and his attitudes change. As difficulty increases or discouragement creeps in, worship keeps his perspective focused on God.

What actions and attitudes characterize a worshiper? How does one worship? Worship is sensing Christ's presence, lifting Him up, exalting Him, responding to Him, with hearts filled with praise and thanksgiving, ready to respond in obedience. Again, worship is an attitude that can be communicated. And our Christian "product" must be exposed to genuine worship if he is to be a dynamic, credible ambassador of Jesus Christ. Filled to overflowing with praise and gratitude for his God, *a worshiper witnesses by the simple spillage of the bounty of his heart.*

Instead of worshiping, many leaders schedule "worship services" hoping that architecture, robes, pipe organs, and stained-glass voices create an emotional tremor which will crack the spiritual ice. Somehow God seems to get lost among the props.

Worship takes place when we shift our focus from the printers ink to the Prince of Peace. It is a movement from contemplation of God to communion with Him. Unless the actual Person of God is sensed and responded to, genuine worship does not take place.

A body of believers has an important role in communicating worship. It must be remembered that worship has both a *context* and *content*. As to *context,* it can take place anywhere. *Content,* factual information about the person and work of God, comes largely (though not exclusively) from two sources: the written Word and the experience of "living epistles." This brings us back to the first two factors of teaching and fellowship. To worship effectively, then, I need exposure to God's *Word* and God's *people.*

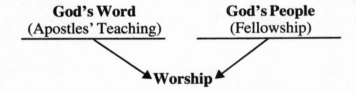

God's Word
(Apostles' Teaching)

God's People
(Fellowship)

Worship

Healthy worship is the product of healthy teaching and healthy fellowship. Healthy teaching systematically works through the whole counsel of God. As the pastor exposes his people to God's attributes and character, His marvelous plan of salvation, His actions in history, and His promises for present day living, the believer is prepared to respond in worship. Provision for fellowship allows believers to identify the presence and work of God in their present experience. Consequently, we rejoice together because of who He is, and the great things He has done. We praise Him as believers openly sharing His work on their behalf. We worship as evidence of His continued faithfulness builds to a crescendo and we acknowledge His Person and presence. When we gather a "mighty army" on Sunday morning, our worship can be genuine because our fellowship with Him and His children has been authentic during the week.

Serving That Sacrifices

Finally, the Spirit of God builds healthy bodies by using believers who are ready for service. "Selling their possessions and goods, they gave to anyone as he had need. . . . And the Lord added to their number daily. . ." (Acts 2:45,47). Mark it well, friend, the non-Christian *saw beauty*. They saw uncommon responses and experienced unusual care and concern. Because of believers' Christ-like attitudes and their sacrificial love, they enjoyed the favor of ALL the people, and God *added to their number daily*. They were candidates for the blessing of God! God was delighted to put new babies in this healthy incubator.

A caring, loving will to serve is basic to evangelism because it provides credibility for the message of the gospel. The church community that reaches out to serve, to give, to sacrifice, and to care will be effective in evangelism. What kind of person do we want to deploy into the world? A learning, fellowshiping, worshiping, serving individual. Why do Christians not get involved in serving? Maybe it's because their learning is unrelated to life, their fellowship is sterile, and their worship is contrived.

A well-taught, fellowshiping, worshiping person serves automatically. Evangelism for him is not a Tuesday night event; he is on duty twenty-four hours a day. His whole life is a living and willing sacrifice, a sweet savor to God and men. He offers himself as a "living sacrifice" knowing that it is no longer he, but Christ who dwells in him, who reaches out to a needy world. Evangelism is what Christ does through the preaching, fellowship, worship, and service of His bride. Realizing this great fact, the believer presents himself to be an instrument for noble purposes. The qualities of Christ will be built into his life if they are present and honored in the circle of his associations. His personality is a product of his relationship. It is imperative that we now consider the nature of the church, his transforming community.

Chapter 5, Notes

1. James Engel, *Contemporary Christian Communications* (Nashville: Thomas Nelson, Inc., 1979), p. 30.

2. Ibid., p. 31.

3. C. B. Hogue, *Love Leaves No Choice* (Waco, TX: Word Books, 1976), pp. 31-32.

4. Engel, *Contemporary Christian Communications,* p. 238.

5. Bailey E. Smith, *Real Evangelism* (Nashville: Broadman Press, 1978), p. 59.

6. George Hunter III, *The Contagious Congregation* (Nashville: Abingdon Press, 1979), p. 39.

Chapter 6

Evangelism and the Church Body

"**H**umpty Dumpty was pushed." The street philosopher who graced the side of a building with this insight captured a truth we all identify with. Brokenness is a common, deep-seated feeling which haunts all of us at one time or another. We are broken people in a broken world. We await the arrival of the "King's Men" to reassemble us again. Despite their best efforts, we still feel like last year's model. This sensed inadequacy often proves to be a crippling liability if we are not members of a healthy, growing church family.

Fortunately God's mission for us in this world does not wait until the reassembly process is completed. He sends us out into the world as salt and light even as He seasons the salt and trims the wick. Healthy believers recognize the growth process as a natural one and welcome each other as church members who are *all* (pastor and board members, too) under construction.

THE PURPOSES OF A HEALTHY CHURCH

If the person we deploy out into the world is going to be effective as salt and light, then he must be the product of a church which takes beauty seriously. In Chapter 5 we discussed the question of

115

the kind of person we want to deploy into the world. The next logical question for discussion is *"What kind of Church makes possible that kind of person?"*

Question One:	What kind of person do we want to deploy into the world?
Question Two:	**What kind of church makes possible that kind of person?**

This second question is critical because *we become like the people we associate with*. Building on the qualities of the "Acts 2 Christian" (Chapter 5) we can project the necessary functions of a healthy church which produce healthy church members. The healthy believer had four qualities: he was a learning, fellowshiping, worshiping, serving person. A balanced diet of these elements produces a wholesome, winsome individual who becomes a candidate for effective witness. Let's take each of these four qualities and relate them to a healthy local church.

To be a learning person who "continues in the apostles' teaching," one's church must be a *learning center*. To be a "fellowshiping person" fully exposed to the giftedness of the body, his church must be a *healing communion*. To be a worshiping person, his church must be a *responding community*. To be significantly involved in service, the church must be a *deploying agency*.

Individual	**Church**
Learning	Learning Center
Fellowshiping	Healing Communion
Worshiping	Responding Community
Serving	Deploying Agency

A LEARNING CENTER

The pastor's role in enabling the church to be an effective learning center cannot be minimized. He serves as both an educator and a model. Both dimensions of his ministry are crucial. Good, regular, systematic biblical teaching programs the mind and heart of the individual and challenges him to respond in obedience to God. Under such teaching, divine boundary conditions are established, God's principles of life are set forth, and His person and work are clearly portrayed. The effective pastor not only presents the concepts and precepts of Scripture, but he relates them specifically and practically to the everyday concerns of life. The possibility of wholesome, positive Christian living is continually reinforced. In his presentation he attempts to paint a verbal portrait of what the individual can *become* and *do* in the light of the biblical truth being presented. Change can come because of the divine provision made available on the believer's behalf. Napoleon was right when he said, "A man becomes the man of his uniform." The effective pastor continually works at visualizing new choices and possibilities for his people as he models these qualities in his own life.

Accepting the fact that it is a sin to bore people with God's Word, the effective pastor is not lazy, but works diligently to present truth with impact. His goal is not to teach the Bible . . . it doesn't need to be taught anything. His purpose is to teach *people* (real, live, breathing, hurting beings) the Bible.

The obedient pastor is to produce the same climate for growth which God produces for His children. Ephesians 3:17 reminds the believer that God has rooted and grounded us in the soil of His love! Not the soil of uncertainty, but the soil of love. He gives us an unqualified "yes" to life by letting us know that we are planted in the soil of His love, and it is this soil from which we are to draw our nourishment and strength. As members of one another, we, too, must function together in love if the body is to become a healing communion. It is the effective, systematic, expository preaching of the Word which provides the context for genuine fellowship.

Generally, the focus of such teaching should be edification, not evangelism. An altar call every Sunday should be carefully rethought in the light of Scripture and church history. As a general rule, the "church gathered" comes together to be "built up" in the faith. The "church scattered" is to be involved in evangelism. It may come as a surprise to many to discover that the altar call, like the Sunday school, is of recent origin. One may read thousands of pages of church history without discovering a reference to such a practice before the last century. It is, in fact, a unique development of American protestantism.

> It has no clear precedent in the traditional worship of the Reformation, or even in the spiritual exercises in the protestant revival movements in the seventeenth or early eighteenth centuries. Neither the Puritans, the Pietists, nor the Methodists, all of whom figured so prominently in setting the pattern for spiritual life of early America, had an intrinsic notion of 'the altar call' in their public order of worship.[1]

Whatever else could be said, the altar call (not taught in Scripture) should be used wisely and with integrity in relationship to the text of Scripture and the minds of men.

A HEALING COMMUNION

Fellowship reinforces the truth taught and links it with personal experience for added impact. As an educator, the pastor must understand and acknowledge the educational implications of fellowship. The believer challenged by the preached Word on Sunday morning can find counsel and support for implementation of the truth if vital fellowship experiences are a regular part of the church life. The reservoir of truth, filled on Sunday morning, must become a river of blessing during the week. It is in the context of fellowship (body life) that the giftedness of the entire body is most capable of functioning. The father struggling with the discipline of his children may discover the *need* for a biblical approach on Sunday morning and get *specifics* from other members during the week as he shares his concerns with them. Getting these specifics involves being exposed to the counsel and concern (giftedness) of others. And there is no substitute for the real life, down-to-earth sharing of truth as it is experienced in everyday living.

At Mariners Church, where I served as pastor, we had dozens of groups of men meeting weekly to share their life in Christ together. Much healing took place as these men shared (1) the *Word* and *prayer,* (2) their *schedules,* and (3) their *relationships.* Meeting in supportive groups of three or four, they became catalysts to one another's spiritual growth as they held each other accountable in specific areas of their lives. Important schedule items (critical appointments, decisions, etc.) were shared as prayer requests. Relationship concerns were communicated regularly. For example, it was not unusual to set aside ten to fifteen minutes for personal consideration of our wives' social, emotional, mental, physical, and spiritual needs. Having written down needs in each area, the men would identify the two or three most urgent needs and share their plans to meet them that week. Held accountable to follow through, the men did so, and found growth was the happy result.

Accountability is an important key to growth. In reality, it's the key to Weight-Watchers. Their scales, diets, and exercises are probably not superior to any other weight loss clinic. It's a regular group session which includes a weigh in that gets the weight off. Accountability is so often missing. Where it is present, growth inevitably follows. Wives would come to me and say, "Joe, I don't know what's going on in those groups, but keep it up!" Simply stated, the men were learning how to love each other, and the skills are transferable! It is doubtful such learning could take place Sunday morning, no matter how eloquent the pastor may be. Home Bible studies provide another significant context for the experience of vital fellowship. In such groups, needs can be shared, experiences communicated, and gifts can be exercised in such a way that real growth and healing take place.

Unfortunately, the very dynamics which cause growth are killed by growth. In the beginning stages everyone knows everyone and each family contributes in a meaningful way to the ongoing ministry of the fellowship. Everyone feels needed and important. But numerical growth tends to depersonalize relationships and dilute fellowship. This leaves the growing church with the task of decentralization, a function accomplished by encouraging and providing for vital fellowship experiences in a small group setting.

Believers need to meet together as a mighty army in celebration and worship, but they also need to be a part of a small band of men or women where supportive fellowship can be a reality. Only then is the church freed to be a healing communion.

The responsible church leader must examine the programming of his church in light of his people's need for vital fellowship. In many cases, the church has lost all sight of body function and has made the forms (programs) sacred. Success is often measured on the basis of whether or not a particular program has grown numerically, rather than on its contribution to the free flow of the giftedness of the body. For example, how can we say we are committed to strengthening the family when our church programs often separate the family, taking parents away from spending time with their children? Pastors often cannot believe it when I tell them I was at home six nights of each week as pastor of a very large church. A biblical philosophy of ministry makes such an option a possibility.

A RESPONDING COMMUNITY

Sound teaching and healthy fellowship set the stage for worship. The healthy church is a *responding community* in which God "inhabits the praise of His people." The joy of relationship leads the family to the triumphal celebration and worship of their heavenly Father. Growing in love with Him, captivated by His grace, His people respond in obedience and service. When the spiritual life of a congregation is weak, it is most evident at the level of worship. In a positive sense, the vitality of the church is best indicated by the nature of its worship. Programs, budgets, facilities, and numbers can be deceiving.

God is seeking those who will worship Him in spirit and truth. Such worship leads to commitment and service. "Worship expresses itself in witness; witness fulfills itself in worship. The unifying theme is the glory of God and of His Christ, and there is a great need for this to be the Supreme incentive of our modern evangelism."[2] Worship which does not produce witness is hypocrisy.

"Worship that is pleasing to God will inevitably send us out to bear witness of the Name we have sought to honor."[3]

A DEPLOYING AGENCY

Motivated by sound teaching, encouraged and equipped by the body, God's children lift up their eyes unto the fields ripe for harvest. The vision of service is constantly cultivated by a teaching, fellowshiping, and worshiping family. On a recent trip to California I was delighted to hear that Los Gatos Christian Church has nearly 200 young people who have committed themselves to vocational Christian service. A healthy fellowship, undergirded by good teaching and joyful worship, produces committed disciples!

What we are saying is that the beautification of the bride is a balanced process involving teaching, fellowship, worship, and service. This process, *edification,* is dependent upon the *proper functioning* of each individual part of the body (Ephesians 4:16-17). Ultimately, the edification (building up) of the bride is dependent upon Christ, who "nourishes and cherishes" her so that she may be spotless and without wrinkle. Christ, the head of the body (the bride), orchestrates the functioning of each individual part as it utilizes its special gift for the betterment of the corporate body. He nourishes His bride by leading her into growth-producing teaching, fellowship, and worship experiences.

As we noted earlier, the long term result of this process is a holy character and a blameless conduct. These qualities, engraved by Christ's Spirit into living beings, make Christians living epistles read by all men. It is His desire that they become suitable reading material. As stated earlier, Christ works *directly* through the church's *message* (kerygma), its *fellowship* (koinonia), and its worship and service (diakonia) to draw men unto Himself.[4] It is the drama of redemption as it is taught, lived, and experienced which gives evangelism its impact. It is important to see that evangelism is not something we do for Christ; it is something He does through us.

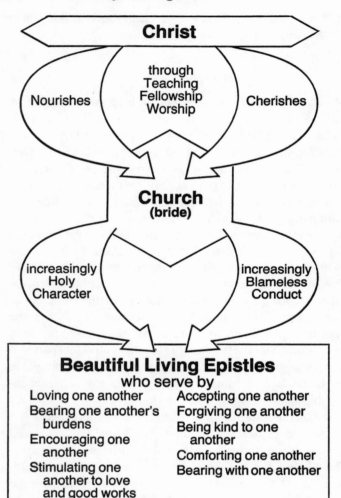

The critical question is "What are nonbelievers reading?" Is the message music to their ears? Arnold Toynbee once stated that "most people have not rejected Christianity, but a caricature." How tragic that many have rejected Christ because the bride was not very Christlike. Like real people, the body of Christ has its diseases which tend to turn away rather than attract.

TO BE AVOIDED LIKE THE PLAGUE

The New Testament reveals four leavens which are to be avoided in the corporate life of the body. They are evangelism killers. Their presence in the body is ugly, and contaminates the reputation of the bride. To produce the kind of church which deploys beautiful people out into a lost world, these leavens must be eliminated. In Matthew 16:6-12 our Lord instructs His disciples to beware of the leaven (the evil influence) of the Pharisees and Sadducees. These warnings are given to the future founders of His bride, the church. The Lord warns them against allowing the beliefs of the Pharisees and Sadducees to influence (leaven) the life and fellowship of the church. The leaven of the Pharisees is *hypocrisy*. The leaven of the Sadducees is *rationalism*. Paul warns of the leaven of *impurity* in 1 Corinthians 5 and the leaven of *legalism* in Galatians 5.

Four Marks of Ugliness
Enemies of Effective Evangelism

Hypocrisy	Matthew 16
Rationalism	Matthew 16
Impurity	1 Corinthians 5
Legalism	Galatians 5

These diseases eliminate effective service, destroy worship, distort fellowship, and cripple evangelism. As such, they produce crippled, inconsistent, hypocritical "living epistles . . . read of all men."

The Spreading of Hypocrisy

The leaven of the Pharisees is *religious externalism or hypocrisy*. When such a disease prevails, church members get caught up in ritual without reality, motion without meaning. The word "hypocrite" comes from a Greek word which literally means to "speak from under a mask." In the Greek theater actors were often called "hypocrites" because they wore masks. The term came to refer to someone who was phony, who said one thing and did something else.

Pharisees were "keepers of the old wineskins." They were upset with Christ because He didn't go along with the "games Pharisees play." Christ's followers dismayed them by eating with dirty hands and picking grain on the Sabbath. The Pharisees would have loved to enroll Christ and His disciples in a "finishing school" where they would learn how to launder their lives, bleaching out any evidence of contact with "publicans and sinners." The Pharisees, self-appointed fruit inspectors, were quick to establish spiritual "pecking orders" based on external performance rather than internal character qualities. As such, they produced tremendous pressure upon their contemporaries to conform to cultural standards which they had established, most of which were not biblical. I hope some of the parallels are obvious.

In 1 Timothy 1:5 Paul tells Timothy that love, the ultimate aim of ministry, is possible when men are freed from hypocrisy. The verse reads, "The goal of this command is love, which comes from a pure heart and a good conscience and a sincere faith." The term "sincere" is actually the word "hypocrite" with the Greek letter alpha in front of it. It could be translated "unhypocritical." Note it carefully, friend, that love, the ultimate expression of God's presence, springs from a *pure heart*, a *clear conscience*, and a *life free of hypocrisy*. Man's heart and conscience are part of his inner being and as such are invisible and unknowable to others. All one can observe is an individual's daily walk, his reaction to people and events, and his life style. Man's life style is like the tip of the iceberg; the rest is out of sight under water.

To understand the significance of what Paul is saying to his friend Timothy, let me quote from the surrounding context. "As I urged you when I went into Macedonia, stay there in Ephesus so that you may command certain men not to teach false doctrines any longer nor to devote themselves to myths and endless genealogies. These promote controversies rather than God's work—which is by faith. The goal of this command is love, which comes from a pure heart and a good conscience and a sincere faith. Some have wandered away from these and turned to meaningless talk. They want to be teachers of the law, but they do not know what they are talking about or what they so confidently affirm" (1 Timothy 1:3-7).

Note carefully that Paul is comparing teachers with teachers, ministries with ministries. All would claim to be involved in communicating the truth. Some are teaching false doctrines and seem to feel that their purpose is to be involved in debating issues which result in mere speculation and endless discussion. Paul says that they have missed the whole point of truth. Truth is designed to impact upon life in such a way that it produces love. The goal of instruction is love. This is the measure, the mark, of the mature body of believers. Stating the verse negatively, *an impure heart produces a guilty conscience which results in a phony life style (hypocrisy)*. There is a definite cause-effect relationship between these three elements.

Impurity ———————▶ Guilt ———————▶ Pretense

God, the source of love, seeks human channels through which He can express His love. We are not only "messages to be read" but instruments to be used. But God's love is *contaminated by an impure heart, confined by a guilty conscience*, and *counterfeited by a phony life style*.

Paul is suggesting that the guilt of unconfessed impurity forces one into a retreating, cowering, hiding, fugitive mode of living. This has been true since the Garden. When Adam and Eve sinned, fellowship with God (and each other) was broken and they became fugitives from God and each other. For Adam, it was "the woman thou gavest me" who was blamed for the fall. Eve blamed the serpent. Salvation does not automatically end the fugitive pattern of living. If the leaven of hypocrisy is to be avoided, the church fellowship must adopt the principle that *maturity is always a return to reality* about (1) God, (2) oneself, and (3) others. The maturing person wants to grow and recognizes his need for the input of other members of the body. We've all heard the unbeliever who doubts the sincerity of the local church because of hypocritical church members. We fight embarrassment and shame as he recounts the actions of unethical church leaders and reminds us of immorality in the choir loft, not to mention its inroads into the pastoral study.

To leave hypocrisy behind and grow towards authenticity, we need to develop an openness to *feedback* and *self-disclosure*. Feedback from others provides us with insight about areas of needed growth and development, whether the areas are hidden from self or from others. The Bible says "As iron sharpens iron, so one man sharpens another." If the local church which shapes the lives of those it deploys into the world is going to be a healthy, authentic, redemptive community, feedback among believers must be encouraged. Many have isolated themselves from the giftedness of the body by not being open to feedback. To grow, I must encourage believers to "speak the truth in love" . . . to me. They will not do it unless I encourage and welcome it . . . and that's what maturity is all about.

The counsel, wisdom, and experience of others becomes a resource for me to draw upon *to the degree that I am open to feedback and self-disclosure*. It is my belief that pride is probably the biggest enemy of authenticity. We fear losing the respect of our peers if we disclose that we are less than perfect and are "standing in the need of prayer." But to have deep hurts, blindspots, and areas of inadequacy is not abnormal. It is abnormal—it is a counterfeit existence—when we attempt to cover inadequacy and refuse to deal with areas in which we need help.

A counterfeit is something which purports to be genuine but isn't. Counterfeits are accepted and respected up until the moment their inauthenticity is discovered. At that point their credibility is lost, and their beauty turns to ugliness. Some therefore conclude that any disclosure of imperfection moves one into the camp of the hypocrites. Not so. It is pretending to be perfect, pretending to be adequate, which is hypocritical. Besides, self-disclosure should also be very positive. We need to be able to share our dreams, longings, and desires with a close friend who can give us encouragement, insight, and direction. Acknowledgement of our dependency and inadequacy can be a beautiful and encouraging act. Often the greatest gift we can share is the "gift of our need." If our model Christian, deployed out into the world is to be good news, he must be authentic. Purity of heart, integrity of conscience, and sincerity of life style are essential qualities.

Authenticity, then, is simply *living openly and communicating freely from the context of the present stage of one's pilgrimage towards wholeness.* According to Paul, the ministry focus of a healthy body is threefold: the heart, the conscience, and the life style. The conscience is God's monitoring system. It is a flashing red light on our spiritual dashboard which tells us something is wrong with the engine. Hypocrites put masking tape over the red light and ignore it. Authentic believers, seeking purity and integrity, invite God to perform a white glove inspection of the heart on a regular basis as they respond immediately to God's warning signals. They also welcome feedback from other believers. Regular confession to God and other believers keeps communication channels open and relationships honest and healthy. Our model Christian will have impact if he is part of a church fellowship committed to purity, integrity, and sincerity.

The Spreading of Unbelief

The Sadducees were anti-supernaturalists. They didn't believe in the resurrection or angelic beings. For all practical purposes, they treated the universe as a closed system subject only to natural forces. As an approach to life, rationalism limits human accomplishment to human ability. The term portrays a person who has lost his vision of the sovereignty and providence of God and as a result is incapable of dreaming God-sized goals. Such a philosophy siphons away the divine dimensions of life and reduces Christianity to nothing but a glorified humanism.

Where there is no Spirit-given vision, there can be no effective evangelism. Believers must have their mental vision purged of all temporal, selfish, and limiting concerns. The biblical principle is vision-oriented evangelism. Only a Spirit-inspired vision of both man's lostness and God's available power can lift evangelism from an occasionally scheduled "project" to a total life style.

Men of vision live so all the time. The leaven of the Sadducees destroys vision. It is the epitome of unbelief. Churches afflicted with this disease are constantly checking their spiritual pulses and declaring, "It's useless, it cannot be done." Faith in God's provision is noticeably absent in such congregations. Skepticism, pessimism, and apathy are apparent. The healthy church needs modern giant killers like David and Caleb who are "foolish enough to believe God!"

Many streams of thought feed the rationalistic channel of thinking. Thoughts like, "It's already been tried," or, "It's too risky and might prove to be embarrassing if it doesn't work," stoke the fires of rationalism. An unwillingness to depart from treasured traditions and forms for the sake of antiquity stunts a faith that would reach out in contemporary fashion. And a rationalization of failures or inadequacies as being "the way God would have it" can build a formidable foundation of rationalism in the minds of those who should believe in the God of miracles.

One subtle form of anti-supernaturalism often grows out of a perverted, unbalanced view of God's sovereignty. Some pastors and leaders excuse their lack of effectiveness by running to an explanation that ties itself to His sovereignty. The lack of evidence of supernatural, God-empowered growth and vitality is explained away on the basis of God having willed it. To some it is folly to dream, to reach, to stretch, to plan, to believe and act accordingly. A passive, ho-hum, wait-and-see attitude is not unusual. But *faith* is what pleases God. Not to take the promises of God out of mothballs and by faith apply them to the challenges of life is the ultimate mark of a Sadducee. Our Lord warned us to avoid such evil teaching.

While at Los Gatos Christian Church in California I got the distinct impression that God was alive and in good health! They de-

light in involving themselves to the hilt in projects so big that unless God acts, they are doomed to failure. The people sense it, and
are changed by it. The testimony of God's response to their faith
has touched the whole community. Hundreds have trusted Christ
because of it. It's contagious! When you've got the real disease, it
spreads rapidly down the webs of relationships in a given community.

My friendship through the years with Bill Bright, the founder
and director of Campus Crusade for Christ, has been another lesson in faith. Here is a man who believes God, takes His purposes
seriously, and acts accordingly. I never go away from his presence
without being challenged to believe God in a bigger way. May his
tribe increase! The writer to the Hebrews reminds us that without
faith it is impossible (not possible) to please God (11:6). Our
Acts 2 Christian needs to be surrounded by men and women of
faith and vision.

The Spreading of Impurity

Paul introduces a third deadly leaven in the fifth chaper of
1 Corinthians. It is the leaven of impurity. He writes, "Don't you
know that a little yeast (impurity) works through the whole batch of
dough? Get rid of the old yeast that you may be a new batch without
yeast—as you really are" (1 Corinthians 5:6-7). The proverbial expression: "One bad apple spoils the whole box" is true. Impurity
spreads in a similar manner if it is not checked. All that is coarse,
crude, and carnal must be avoided if a church is to be a candidate
for God's blessing.

> "It is God's will that you should be holy; that you
> should avoid sexual immorality; that each of you should
> learn to control his own body in a way that is holy and
> honorable. . . . For God did not call us to be impure,
> but to live a holy life" (1 Thessalonians 4:3-4, 7).

Love springs from a pure heart. No clever arrangement of rotten
eggs will make a good omelet!

To make purity a reality, every thought must be brought into
captivity to Christ so that He can fill the believer's mind with

"whatsoever is pure. . . ." It is imperative, then, to avoid contamination especially at the level of our thought life. This fact often leads to misunderstanding when it comes to evangelism. At a Pastor's Conference I once was cornered by a pastor who was very upset because I stressed the need to make friends with non-Christian neighbors. He insisted that the Bible taught that we were to love our enemies, but not to be friends with them. The disagreement boiled down to what I considered to be a misunderstanding of the doctrine of separation. Separation is not isolation. It is living a distinctive, pure life in the midst of an impure world. It is being salt and light in the midst of darkness and death. It is being a "living epistle" which is available for others to read. There is no impact without contact, and contact can be risky. Our Lord avoided contamination, yet was accused of being a drunkard, a friend of publicans and sinners. He maintained purity in the midst of impurity.

The healthy church must deal immediately and directly with the disease of impurity. To allow impurity to function like yeast in the body is ecclesiastical suicide. It is from impurity which exists *within* the body of Christ that the believer is to separate himself.

> "I have written you in my letter not to associate with sexually immoral people—not at all meaning the people of this world who are immoral, or the greedy and swindlers, or idolaters. In that case you would have to leave this world.
> But now I *am writing you that you must not associate with anyone who calls himself a brother* but is sexually immoral or greedy, an idolater or a slanderer, a drunkard or a swindler. With such a man do not even eat" (1 Corinthians 5:9-11, italics mine).

It is impurity within the body which destroys the bride's beauty and discredits Christ, the bridegroom. Paul's instruction concerning such impurity is clear. "Clean out the old leaven . . ." he says. Healthy church discipline is a vital part of maintaining the corporate image/testimony of the local church. It serves notice to the community that although the church is a community of imperfect people moving towards wholeness, impurity is not acceptable as a way of life. Difficult as church discipline is, it can be a positive force for evangelism in that it declares to the community that the church intends, by God's grace, to *practice* what it *preaches*. Our Acts 2 Christian needs to be surrounded by people committed to purity.

The Spreading of Legalism

We are all legalists by nature. The church at Galatia fell into the trap of legalism, and Paul had to write to correct this dangerous error. Reminding them of their freedom in Christ he asked them, "You were running a good race; who cut in on you and kept you from obeying the truth?" Legalism is an ethical system which measures spirituality in terms of one's compliance with an arbitrary set of rules. The legalist likes to think he has avoided the problem of "worldliness." Holiness to him is a world-denying withdrawal, a radical otherworldliness. Such a definition seems to totally ignore Paul's comments in Colossians 2:16, 20-22.

> "Therefore do not let anyone judge you by what you eat or drink, or with regard to a religious festival, a New Moon celebration or a Sabbath day. . . . Since you died with Christ to the basic principles of this world, why, as though you still belonged to it, do you submit to its rules: "Do not handle! Do not taste! Do not touch!"? These are all destined to perish with use, because they are based on human commands and teachings."

"Whatever else Paul may be saying to the Colossians and to us, he is saying that worldliness is a legalistic preoccupation with eating and drinking and sabbath keeping. He is saying that worldliness is a legalistic preoccupation with externalities, a legalistic preoccupation with conformity to a man-made code of don'ts."[5] The following quote is a classical illustration of this problem of legalistic preoccupation. "We preach against every form of worldliness including *television, newspapers, smoking, drinking, worldly amusements, improper dress,* and even against coffee, tea, coca-cola, and overeating."[6]

In his attempt to avoid the error of worldliness, the legalist is snared in its very trap. The rules of the legalist are usually cultural in their origin rather than biblical. For example, there are parts of the world where a woman with pierced ears would never be allowed to take communion in her local church, in spite of her redemption in Christ Jesus. Legalism has killed the evangelistic impact of countless churches because legalism is *pure, unadulterated ugliness*. Not only is it ugly; it fails in its purpose.

> "Our young people know how long to wear their hair, how short their skirts should be, that it is wrong to go to the movies; and all the while they are taking drugs and trying to decide about premarital sex. We are often as irrelevant with our set of rules as the oral traditions of the Jews which had a rule for each day."[7]

It seems so much easier to draw up lists and bury ourselves behind self-imposed laws than to come to grips with our freedom in Christ. Like a frontal lobotomy, legalism severs the nerve of life and vitality and leaves its victims breathing but not beautiful. It is a subtle sin, but sin nevertheless.

A legalist is one who would suffer from the following symptoms. He would be a great fence builder with the compulsive need to label, categorize, and sterilize people, places, and things. Like some health food fans, he would not only know what is wrong for him, but unfortunately for everyone else, too. There would be the tendency to act as a self-appointed judge and jury, and assume the role of joy-robber whose prey is the body of Christ. A person with this mental framework would be ineffective in reaching the lost, having constructed barriers based on unbiblical presuppositions about separation. Unlike Paul who "became all things to all men," the legalist is rigid, inflexible, and unbending.

If the church is going to take beauty seriously, it must face ugliness with integrity. To be beautiful, we need to associate with beautiful people. There is an old adage which says that "poor people need to take rich people out to dinner and listen because success leaves clues." Pick out someone in the congregation who has that special "radiance" and spend some time together. Ask yourself what it is that makes your friend distinctive and attractive. If some of your friends are suffering from a severe case of "hardening of the attitudes," perhaps you can be God's instrument to nudge them towards a more balanced, wholesome, authentic life style. Your association with a loving, caring, wholesome, supportive family is the key to your personal beauty and a major factor in your evangelistic effectiveness. Are you part of the solution or the problem? If part of the solution, work hard at eliminating the leavens of hypocrisy, rationalism, impurity, and legalism.

DEVELOP DIVINE SIGNPOSTS

"Eliminate the negative, accentuate the positive" isn't bad advice. Besides eliminating negative diseases, what positive influences should the church be showing and spreading from the overflow of its gathered life?

The New Testament reveals four corporate qualities which let the nonbeliever know that God is revealing Himself in this world. These are *love, unity, good works,* and *hope*. Each of these qualities is singled out for its particular evangelistic impact. When they are observed and "felt" by the non-Christian, something uniquely divine is communicated. In a very real sense they serve as divine signposts for the nonbeliever, signposts which lead him toward the foot of the cross.

> **Divine Signposts**
> 1. Love
> 2. Unity
> 3. Good Works
> 4. Hope

The Display of Love

Defining love is like mental housekeeping in a revolving door. Most of our descriptions are *lexical* in nature, that is, like dictionary definitions. "Love is seeking the highest good of its object" is an example of such a definition. Not too bad, but not very helpful when it comes to explaining love. Sometimes our definitions are *behavioral*. Love is washing dishes, or cleaning the sink, or scrubbing the tub. Not too romantic, but *realistic* and *observable*. Occasionally we communicate experiential definitions of love such as, "I feel loved when you listen, when you spend time with me, when you forgive me," etc. Our Lord said, "All men will know that you are my disciples if you love one another" (John 13:35). Notice several important principles growing out of Christ's remarkable statement.

First, love is more than a "warm glow" somewhere inside. It is an observable, tangible phenomenon which takes place between people. When love acts it can be seen, felt, and experienced by others as object or observer.

Second, love as seen, felt, and experienced is somehow linked with Christ in the mind of the nonbeliever. "All men will know that you are my disciples if you love. . . ." A genuine love relationship focuses the nonbeliever's attention in the right direction! It probably is the key factor in changing the nonbeliever from a negative to a positive attitude towards the gospel. When the Spirit of God writes the script, growing, loving relationships are the result. When the unbeliever reads that kind of a script, he recognizes its divine authorship.

Third, love can be chosen or shunned by the believer—it is not a guaranteed attitude for one who has chosen Christ. All men will know . . . if. *If* you have love for one another. Over and over again the New Testament writers exhort, admonish, and warn believers about the necessity of love. The opposites of love are not very attractive. We will discuss some practical means of expressing love in a later chapter. Our model Christian, deployed into the world, must be part of a loving, caring community if he is to be effective in evangelism.

The Display of Unity
Unity is another divine signpost for our non-Christian friends. It, like love, focuses their attention in the right direction.

God, as it were, surfaces and becomes visible when believers dwell together in unity. Paul's instructions in Ephesians 4:2-3 link love and unity together. "Be completely humble and gentle; be patient, bearing with one another in love. Make every effort to keep the unity of the Spirit through the bond of peace." John 17 records our Lord's prayer for His bride. "May they be brought to complete unity to let the world know that you sent me and have loved them even as you have loved me" (John 17:23).

Note that when a local assembly is characterized by unity, the world observes two important facts. First, the remarkable, distinctive quality of unity communicates to them that God sent Christ! Genuine unity apparently is such a rare commodity that when disciples of Christ have it, an observer concludes Christ is a man sent from God Himself. Notice carefully that Christ prays for *unity*, not *uniformity*. Where there are great pressures for uniformity one should be suspicious. Christians do not have to look, dress, think, and act alike. The church is not an assembly line producing only Fords. If a church has genuine unity, it isn't overly concerned with uniformity. Most of the pressures for uniformity focus around cultural rather than biblical issues, although many who push for uniformity *assume* they are biblical issues.

Biblical unity also encourages a healthy diversity which is essential for beauty and authenticity. The creative genius of the Holy Spirit has endowed His creatures with an amazing diversity of gifts, abilities, talents, and cultural distinctives. Salvation does not destroy such diversities; rather it redeems and enhances them, bringing them under the Lordship of Christ.

Legalism is the great enemy of unity because it assumes unity means uniformity. When "unity" is obtained in a legalistic community, its members usually become cult-like zombies, stripped of the individual sparkle of true Christian vitality. The corporate life style becomes very bland, tasteless, and contrived. When the beauty of the Christ who refused to be bottled in "old wineskins" is replaced with Pharisaical legalism, evangelistic effectiveness is greatly impaired.

Our model Christian needs to be part of a fellowship marked by unity. Church fights, family feuds, power plays, politicking, and manipulation are not qualities which attract men and women to Christ. Many "spiritual banty roosters" need to get their wings clipped!

The Display of Good Works

Believers are "created in Christ Jesus to do good works, which God prepared in advance for us to do" (Ephesians 2:10). Good works are also a powerful tool for evangelism. The beneficial, helpful, supportive, encouraging, sacrificial actions of believers in their areas of influence become significant signposts for the nonbeliever. "Live such good lives among the pagans that, though they accuse you of doing wrong, they may see your good deeds and glorify God on the day he visits us" (1 Peter 2:12). To say that they will see our good works presupposes activity. The Spirit-filled Christian is a busy person, actively engaged in the business of the King. Evangelism involves active, diligent effort.

The New Testament pattern of evangelism is a blend of proclamation and practical meeting of needs. The hungry were fed, the sick ministered to, the naked clothed, and the widows and fatherless cared for. The music of the believers' selfless actions became the platform for the words of the gospel. The world, observing this care, commented on their love for each other. Thousands of believers willingly marched into Alexandria, Egypt, during the plague and gave their lives to minister to the dying. Many sold themselves into slavery in the salt mines so they could minister to fellow believers held in bondage, never again to see the light of day. As the Roman persecutions grew in intensity, long lines of chained Christians were dragged to Rome for execution. Christians from local villages walked with them, ministering to their physical and spiritual needs. Their presence often turned these tragic, beastly marches into triumphal processions.

The bottom line is that you and I should excel at meeting needs through our good works. We are created by God for the purpose of *doing good works!* Good works are simply practical expressions of love. We know that faith without works is dead faith. Genuine faith produces a life style characterized by good works. Our love is to find practical, tangible expression in and through the actions of our lives. As we do this, the good news is translated into deeds. It is good news when a drunkard is loved up out of his alcoholic hell. It is good news when an adulterous husband is restored to his wife and family. It is good news when Christians adopt the fatherless and care for the abandoned and hopeless. It is divine music when believers apply what they profess to the hurts, pains, and sorrows of mankind.

The Holy Spirit has gifted each of us with abilities which are channels for His love to become operational towards both the Christian and non-Christian community. These abilities include what is normally called "spiritual gifts" as well as special skills such as carpentry, plumbing, cooking, gardening, etc. I am certain God has used my gift of teaching as a vehicle for good works. I also know that He has used my abilities with a hammer, saw, and nails to win some neighbors to Christ. My wife's cooking abilities have been the channel through which God's love has been felt by numerous non-Christian neighbors, many of whom have become believers.

A community of believers, freed by the Spirit to live beyond selfishness, becomes increasingly powerful to witness as it makes good works a way of life. First Baptist Church of Winlock, Washington, helped purchase a paramedic rescue vehicle for their local community. Their "good works" are well-known in the community. At the same time, they are bursting at the seams. The First Southern Baptist Church of Del City, Oklahoma, was deeply disturbed because of an x-rated theatre near the church, purchased the theatre and now uses it to show Christ-centered movies. On Sunday afternoons as many as six hundred children are exposed to the gospel through a free movie and Bible lesson. Our "deployed Christian" needs to be part of a church family known and respected for its good works.

The Display of Hope

"Always be prepared to give an answer to everyone who asks you to give the reason for the hope that you have" (1 Peter 3:15). Hope is another divine signpost which captures the attention of the nonbeliever living in his despair-filled world. Children of the King must not allow the world's pessimism to poison their heritage of hope. Christians and non-Christians share life's tragedies, sorrows, and hurts. But, we "sorrow not as others who have no hope." The nonbeliever who observes the Christian facing life's trials with a sense of hope and optimism is going to want to know what it is that creates such a response. Peter says he will ask you the reason for your hope. Notice carefully that the underlying premise of Peter's whole discussion is a relationship or association with the non-Christian which is significant enough that hope has a serious chance of being observed. Hope is most powerful when it is observed against the backdrop of seeming hopelessness. When the non-Christian is allowed to share in some of these experiences, the music of the gospel plays loud and clear.

But hope is not simply a temporary response to difficult circumstances. It is also a permanent, settled attitude toward life. Biblical theology makes it clear that there is no room for an attitude of pessimism to rule in the life of God's children. The "deployed Christian" needs to surround himself with hope-filled, optimistic believers. The magnetic power of hope stands as an intriguing possibility for the searching nonbeliever. Could it be that he, too, could discover a reason to be filled with hope?

Love, unity, good works, and hope are divine signposts which the beautiful bride wears as apparel, calling attention to her divine lineage. They contrast sharply with the diseases of hypocrisy, unbelief, impurity, and legalism which weaken an ailing church. But the signposts awaken the passerby to a healthy church which produces learning, fellowshiping, worshiping, serving members—God's medicine for a sick world. The healthy church members which fill healthy church bodies aren't in good shape by accident. They are led into a life style of health. By whom? This question will be answered in the next chapter.

Chapter 6, Notes

1. Robert E. Coleman, "The Origin of the Altar Call in American Methodism," *Asbury Seminarian* (Winter 1958): 19.

2. John R. Stott, *Our Guilty Silence* (Grand Rapids: Eerdmans, 1969), p. 27.

3. Ibid., p. 25.

4. George Hunter III, *The Contagious Congregation* (Nashville: Abingdon Press, 1979), p. 28.

5. Vernon Grounds, "Loving the World: Rightly or Wrongly," *Christianity Today,* April 4, 1980, p. 20.

6. Dr. Peter S. Ruckman, "More Baloney from BJU," *Bible Believers' Bulletin* (July 3, 1980):1.

7. Dr. Thomas Dollar, *Baptist Bulletin,* February 1980, p. 1.

Chapter 7

Evangelism and the Church Leadership

*T*he machined precision, quality materials, and excellent crafts-manship which go into a Weatherby rifle make it a thing of beauty . . . at least to me. For years I have respected the Weatherby name and tradition. All the evidence I could accumulate from magazines, journals, and personal recommendations confirmed the excellence of the product. Weatherby has done its "pre-evangelism" well. The "music" of Weatherby is very good. Its products have such integrity they sell themselves. For example, in 1976 they produced a limited number of the Weatherby Bi-Centennial edition which sold out before any advertising reached the marketplace.

One day a young man named Ed Weatherby started attending Mariners Church. Imagine the pleasure of discovering that he was part of the famed Weatherby tradition. Roy Weatherby—*the* Roy Weatherby—is his father. The day he took me through the Weatherby plant I thought I'd died and gone to heaven. I met his father, sat in his trophy-filled office, and talked enthusiastically about their famous products. There is something to be learned from the Weatherby tradition.

Notice that when the consumer hears the "music" of the rifle he is gradually prepared to succumb and put his money on the line. Weatherby's greatest emphasis has been on *quality assurance* and

141

quality control; and the rifle sells itself. There is no better marketing than a satisfied customer!

If our local churches are to be beautiful, wholesome expressions of the Bride of Christ, someone must devote himself to *quality assurance* and *quality control*. Quality assurance concerns itself with *defining* quality, and then *devising* a strategy to produce it. Quality control is concerned with the *maintenance* of quality once it is assured. Quality is not an accident. The church which deploys into the community wholesome, winsome believers has leadership which takes quality seriously.

This leads us to the consideration of our third question about an evangelistically effective church: *What Kind of Leadership Team Makes Possible that Kind of Church?* Let's review our previous questions.

Question One:	What kind of person do we want to deploy into the world?
Question Two:	What kind of church makes possible that kind of person?
Question Three:	**What kind of leadership team makes possible that kind of church?**

The first question is attempting to *define a product* in terms of qualities which assure its maximum effectiveness. Since our model Christian is the product of the kind of church he attends, the second question is an attempt to *discuss a process* which will assure a quality product. Our third question focuses on a prototype *pattern* or behavioral model which illustrates through example the way in which the corporate body is to function—and then makes sure that quality pattern is produced.

LEADERSHIP: A QUICK LOOK AT THE WHOLE CHURCH

The leadership team is literally a microcosm of the body. They are the prototype, the "mini-church," for the rest of the congregation. Depending on church polity, the leaders are usually called either elders or deacons. "Leadership team" refers to the corporate church leadership regardless of the particular title. *The life style of leadership determines the life style of the body which in turn determines the life style of the one deployed into the world.*

Loving, caring, authentic Christian communities are not produced by church board members who sow discord and strife. And so the quality of relationships between board members may be one of the most critical factors in the church's evangelistic impact. Wherever I go to speak at pastors conferences, I hear a recurring theme: The board can't get along, they're feuding, they're manipulating and seeking their own interests. It is not unusual to find board members in direct opposition to each other and the pastor.

When leaders lack genuine unity, they poison the body and hinder evangelistic effectiveness. If the leaders are not characterized by an obvious love and support for each other, there is little chance for such qualities to be present in corporate fellowship. It's the old story; if you want people to bleed, you've got to hemorrhage. Knowing that "precept begins, but example accomplishes," leaders must strive to be worthy models to follow. Remember our Lord's statement. When a pupil is fully taught, when a man is fully discipled, *he will be like* his teacher. The behavorial model for the congregation is the leadership team. Paraphrasing John 13:35 we could say that "the congregation will know for certain that the church leaders are true disciples of Christ (and therefore worthy models to follow) if they have love for one another." Note the built-in beauty of love's operational definition as described by Paul in 1 Corinthians 13. Imagine the power and the impact for change when leaders relate in this manner (I have substituted the word "leader" for "love" to help make the point):

> The leader is so patient and so kind;
> He never boils with jealousy;
> He never boasts, is never puffed with pride,
> He does not act with rudeness, or insist on his rights;
> He never gets provoked, He never harbors evil thoughts;
> He is never glad when wrong is done,

But always glad when truth prevails;
He bears up under everything,
He exercises faith in everything
He keeps up hope in everything

> (1 Corinthians 13:4-7; adapted from Williams
> Translation of the New Testament)[1]

THE NECESSITY OF MODELING BY LEADERSHIP

Peter underscores the necessity of modeling as he writes,

"I beg the elders among you, be shepherds of the flock
of God that is among you, not as though you had to but
of your own free will, not from the motives of personal
profit but freely, and not as domineering over those in
your charge *but proving yourselves models for the* flock
to imitate."

> (1 Peter 5:1b-3, Williams)

The word "model" can also be translated "pattern," "standard," or
"example." Paul uses the same term when he encourages Timothy
(pastor of the church at Ephesus) to "set an example for the believers in speech, in life, in love, in faith and in purity" (1 Timothy
4:12).

The implications of Peter's words deserve careful consideration. Sheep need shepherds who assume responsibility for the wel-
fare of the flock. Another implication is that shepherds are not to
minister under duress because they have to, but because they freely
choose to care for others. The issue is not skill, gift, or experience,
but rather desire. The leader must like people. He, an under-
shepherd, is to love the sheep as Christ the Great Shepherd does.
He's in the *people* business, not the *church* business. The shepherd
knows his sheep. He calls them by name and they follow him. A
third implication is that the leader (shepherd) serves with no motive of personal profit or gain. Unfortunately, some go out into the
ministry to do good, and end up doing very well. I think you know

what I mean. The position is not to be sought as a status symbol or mark of prestige. It is an opportunity to serve others, committing oneself to their growth, recognition, and achievement.

A fourth principle derived from Peter's statement is that the leader (shepherd) does not pull rank to accomplish his purposes. He leads by example. He is not to domineer or "lord it over" those in his charge. The pattern of the business world with its emphasis on *position power* is not an acceptable model for local church leadership. Our Lord taught this same truth in Luke 22 where he said, "The kings of the Gentiles lord it over them; and those who exercise authority over them call themselves Benefactors. *But you are not to be like that*. Instead, the greatest among you should be like the youngest, and the one who rules like the one who serves. . . . But I am among you as one who serves" (Luke 22:25-26, 27b, italics mine). This same Christ, the head of the church, loved her and *gave himself up for her* so that she could advance towards beauty and royalty (Ephesians 5:25-27).

A fifth conclusion from Peter is that the principle of imitation presupposes the existence of a prescribed, distinctive, God-given way of life (life style). Detailed descriptions of the qualities and characteristics of the leader, our behavioral model, can be found in 1 Timothy 3 and Titus 1. These passages reveal the kind of leadership necessary to produce a beauty parlor which actually produces beauty. The rest of the chapter will develop these important qualifications.

Finally, because the leader leads by example, he must live intentionally. It must be said of him that he "lived a purposeful, distinctive life among believers for their sake" (1 Thessalonians 1:5b, Williams). What we are saying is that effective church leaders *choose* to live and relate to each other in specific, observable, and agreed upon ways. They schedule quality time together because quality relationships take time. Our church board met twice each week because we were committed to the fact that the quality of our relationships was the key to the relationships in our church family. We could not expect our people to develop caring, supportive, redemptive relationships if we didn't. We had no choice if we were going to take beauty seriously. Intentional living also involves such things as mutual accountability, regular involvement in personal ministry, and an ongoing mutual discipleship.

New Testament Qualifications for Leadership

Elders (leaders) are examples to follow; as such, followers are to become like their leaders. In a very real sense they are to talk like their leaders, love like their leaders, care for others like their leaders, build relationships like their leaders, and love and obey God like their leaders. A clear portrait of what the "example to follow" is all about is given in 1 Timothy 3:1-7, Titus 1:5-10, and 1 Peter 5:2. It should be noted that the over twenty qualities listed in the New Testament do not merely apply to church leaders. Instead, they are marks which will characterize every mature child of God. Biblical revelation verbalizes the qualities for the body of Christ. The leader visualizes (incarnates) them.

In an earlier chapter we noted that effective communication had three qualities: ethos, pathos, and logia. *Ethos* focuses on moral and ethical qualities. Sympathy and empathy come from the root *pathos* and focus on caring qualities. *Logia* is a reference to the communicator's verbal abilities. Ethos and pathos are qualities which can be observed and experienced. It is from the presence or absence of ethos and pathos that an opinion is formed about the messenger. If I by personal observation and experience have concluded that the messenger is ethical and caring, I am much more likely to listen to his message (logia). Furthermore, the impact of the message will be much greater if it has been reinforced and undergirded by ethos and pathos. It is important that the messenger *be* good news before he *shares* good news.

Note in the following list that nearly all of the characteristics are ethos and pathos qualities. As you read the list, imagine that you are a nonbeliever who is fortunate enough to have a growing friendship with a Christian having these qualities.

Combined List of Qualifications
(1 Timothy 3:1-7; Titus 1:5-10; 1 Peter 5:2)

Above reproach (good reputation)	One who manages his own family
Husband of one wife	Not a recent convert
Temperate	A good reputation with the nonbeliever
Self-controlled	Not overbearing
Respectable	Loves what is good
Hospitable (lover of strangers)	Upright
Able to teach	Devout
Not given to much wine	Holds firmly to the trust-worthy message
Not violent, but gentle	Not quick-tempered
Not quarrelsome	Not a lover of money

Quality: Giving the Right Response

There are at least four categories of qualities illustrated in this list. First, there are those qualities which have to do with a believer's *responses*. For example, he is to be temperate, not quick-tempered, self-controlled, not violent, but gentle, not quarrelsome or over-bearing. A response is a reaction to circumstances and people. Under favorable conditions, most people probably meet these re-quirements. The real test, however, is how the individual responds to stress.

When the non-Christian observes a believer responding to pressure and pain with a spirit-controlled response, he is seeing God at work in human experience. Stephen's response to stoning caught the attention of a man named Saul! Lack of self-control is dangerous. "Just as untaught men leave the Body wounded and bleeding, undisciplined shepherds by their very example, lead God's flock into treacherous territory, causing unstable sheep to stumble and fall. That's why Paul warned his colleagues not to appoint leaders who have a glaring lack of self-control over their personal and social lives."[2]

I do not intend to comment on all the qualities, but I cannot pass up gentleness. A leader is not to be violent, but gentle. This quality is exactly opposite of the person who feels he has to stand up for every letter of his legal rights. The gentle person backs away from the letter of the law to preserve its spirit. He stays within the limits of that which is moderate and orderly. The Greek term is often used of the condescension of a superior to an inferior. Gentleness is a true measure of one's spiritual maturity. The violent, divisive person is to be warned and then isolated. Never put a critical, divisive person in leadership. He hasn't earned such a right regardless of his training or experience.

Quality: Forming the Right Relationships

A second category of qualities has to do with relationships, to people and to things. A person's relationship to money is perhaps one of the most accurate gauges of his spiritual maturity. God does not want tightwads in places of leadership. Neither the hoarding skinflint nor the wheeling, dealing, fast buck artist is qualified for leading the flock. Imagine the impact a godly, non-materialistic person makes in this materialistic world. God desires that believers give generously and cheerfully of their substance. *The person who is selfish in the area of material things cannot be giving in interpersonal relationships*. The emotional ice of selfishness must be broken before the water of life can flow freely to other thirsty souls. The insatiable desire for money must be brought under scriptural limits.

A one-wife kind of man has eyes for no other woman than the one he married. There is no room for a sensual ladies man on a leadership team. Many men have never divorced their wives or been "unfaithful," but they are not one-women men, and their wives know it. The mature man is faithful to his wife in his imagination as well as his actions.

Our behavioral model is also to be someone who manages his own family well. The Greek word for "well" is *kalos,* which is often translated "beauty," or "good." It is the same term used in verse 7 of Timothy 3 where Paul says the elder must be of good reputation. Our Lord uses it to refer to the good seed (the sons of the king) which he plants in the world. God wants to give visibility to husbands and fathers who manage their family *well* (beautifully). God is interested in *how* the leader relates to his family, not just the *fact* of it. The husband's authority, like Israel's kings, is established by God. Yet most Old Testament kings did not manage Israel well, and it is said of many that they "did evil in the sight of the Lord continuously."

As Frank Accardy puts it, the New Testament leader must be "family proven." If he cannot manage beautifully at home, don't let him get close to leadership in the church. Life's most crucial curriculum is taught in the home. It is not without reason that the world asks, "Is there life after marriage?" The greatest challenges, the greatest pressures we face are behind the front door! The home is an excellent proving ground for the church because both are families. To rule well means to use authority wisely, recognizing that it is derived from God and is a sacred stewardship—not a right. Our leader is never to "lord it over the flock," just as a husband is not to "lord it over" his wife. The Old Testament kings who abused authority failed because they were not in total submission to Jehovah, their head. Submission to Christ provides the necessary checks and balances upon the exercise of authority. Without such submission, leadership produces resentment and bitterness.

As far as his relationship to God is concerned, the leader is not to be a *recent convert*. Our word neophyte comes from this Greek term. In the Greek translation of the Old Testament, the Septuagint, our word "new convert" is translated "newly planted" (cf. Job 14:9, Psalms 128:3, 144:4, Isaiah 5:7). How often we are tempted to put the "newly planted" along with their life and vitality into the leadership limelight. But God is concerned about the quality of the leader's relationship to Him. So many of these new converts go up like a rocket and come down like a rock. Paul warns that conceit is a hazard for the new convert, causing him to fall under the devil's judgment (1 Timothy 3:6). Paul's concern is focused on the new convert, and what sudden recognition could do to him. Conceit literally means to "raise a smoke or mist" and as a result blur one's vision of himself. Premature promotion often produces a deadly distortion of reality leading to a fall from productive and responsible service.

In the King's business only wounded soldiers (veterans) can lead. They have the patience and endurance for the long haul, and have potential for being worthy models. The new convert cannot model what he has not experienced.

The quality of loving what is good (Titus 1:8) pictures one whose mind and heart are properly focused. The Greek term *philagathos* literally means to have a strong affection for that which is honorable and worthy. Practically speaking, it means to have a strong desire for a worthy, honorable life style and appropriate actions. In our terms, this person has a vital relationship to good things. Such a person loves that which has ethical, moral, and practical goodness. According to Paul, the leader is to (1) set an example by doing good (Titus 2:7), (2) encourage believers to be ready for any good enterprise (Titus 3:1), and (3) teach believers to devote themselves to doing good (Titus 3:14). The leader must be noted for his love of goodness.

Since we become what we love, what we love is the truest indication of our character and our motivation. Where our treasure is, our heart is also. The leader who loves and pursues anything which is tainted, suggestive, impure, or unethical is unworthy as a model for Christlikeness. The direction of a man's life and affections must be firmly and clearly demonstrated before he is considered as a behavioral model for our Acts 2 Christian. If a world is to be reached for Christ, we need a multitude of men and women armed with good works. Leaders must set the pace in this vital Christian grace.

Quality: Building the Right Reputation

A third category of leadership qualities focuses particularly in the area of *reputation*. As such, the leader is to be *above reproach* (1 Timothy 3:2, Titus 1:6-7). Those chosen to wait on tables were required to be men of good reputation (Acts 6:3). Luke said that the brothers "spoke well of" Timothy (Acts 16:2). A person who is above reproach provides no grounds for accusation. He cannot be attacked because of his moral or ethical conduct.

There are no watergates in his life. I do not believe this means a man has never failed, but that his failures have been accepted and dealt with in an honorable, satisfactory manner.

Likewise, a leader is to be *respectable* (1 Timothy 3:2). The word in the Greek is *kosmion* from which we get our word "cosmetics." It literally means "to make order out of chaos." In 1 Timothy 2:9 it is used of modest apparel. The root idea of the term focuses on that which is orderly and functioning properly. Plato uses this term extensively of the citizen who has a well-ordered life in which he quietly and faithfully fulfills the duties which are incumbent upon him. Such a citizen was characterized by a tough minded self-management. Under the Lordship of Christ, our leader must have a godly self-discipline which evidences itself in respectable, honorable behavior. As such, he has credibility with those who know him.

Another critical test of leadership readiness is the reputation which one has with the nonbeliever (1 Timothy 3:7). Paul says it should be good! No man who is known as a corner-cutting, fast-talking, unethical business person has any place in church leadership. Judged by his non-Christian peers, our leader is to receive a good report. His vocabulary must be clean, his concern genuine, his motives honorable, his word good, and his promises true. A man with leadership possibilities has nothing to suppress, as well as being self-disciplined and well spoken of by his non-Christian peers.

Quality: Communicating the Right Revelation

A final category of leadership qualities focuses on the leader's ability to handle divine revelation. He is to "hold firmly to the trustworthy message" (Titus 1:9), and be "able to teach" (1 Timothy 3:2). "Holding firmly" implies a settled conviction about the authority and centrality of Scripture. The leader is to be mature enough that he can use the Word effectively in both exhortation and refutation (Titus 1:9). No novices need apply! To be able to "encourage others by sound doctrine and refute those who oppose it" (Titus 1:9), the leader must have a clear understanding of what Scripture teaches. Being "able to teach" means he should be able to communicate truth in an effective manner. Being "able to teach" means much more than having one's frontal lobe crammed with information. The skillful teacher has the ability to get beyond information to the practical *implications* for everyday living. As such he can use Scripture to solve personal problems. The manner in which he applies Scripture to life becomes very important. He is to teach with authority, but not in an authoritarian manner.

The one who is "able to teach" is one who has learned to communicate truth in a gentle, kind, unquarrelsome way according to 2 Timothy 2:24-25. His teaching does not lead to quarrels and empty disputes. Unteachable, quarrelsome people are to be handled by our leader with kindness, patience, and gentleness. Sheep are to be led—never driven.

I've saved the best until last. Our behavioral model is to be *hospitable* (1 Timothy 3:2, Titus 1:8). The Greek term means a "lover of strangers." We should not forget to extend hospitality to strangers (Hebrews 13:2). Believers are encouraged in the habit of inviting guests home for dinner (Romans 13:13). The big idea is that the home circle is to be an open circle, and this is a requirement for a leader. Why? Because a man having a Spirit-controlled life, who manages his family well, and has a good reputation, is a *living, walking miracle*. He is a revelation of God's truth in the world. Furthermore, when hurting, seeking, searching souls are allowed to share the warmth and love of Christian hospitality, they are hearing the music of the gospel—loud and clear. Here's where our evangelism strategies often break down. Christians can't handle their humanity. They don't know how to be themselves.

> We have not grasped that it really is okay for us to be who we are when we are with non-Christians, even if we do not have all the answers to their questions or if our knowledge of Scripture is limited. We forget that we are called to be witnesses to what we have seen and know, not to what we do not know. The key is obedience, not a Th.D.[3]

When Ruthe and I were at Dallas Seminary we lived in an apartment building full of every possible type of human being. We shared a building with students, homosexuals, prostitutes, bank robbers, mechanics, divorcees, singles . . . you name it, we had it. We determined to befriend, love, and hopefully influence them for Christ. On various occasions I had to break up fights, holding the gladiators under gunpoint until police arrived. On two occasions I arrested sexual perverts. Our lives were threatened. Beer bottles were thrown through our bedroom window in the middle of the night.

In spite of some of these inconveniences, we spent many hours with these people. They would eat with us, often bringing their beer cans and ash trays. We tried to take at least one couple out to dinner each week. Our home circle was an open circle and they came, they laughed, they cried, they listened, they watched, they talked, and some were saved. They heard the music and asked about the words. At Youngbloods' Fried Chicken Restaurant, Bettye asked, "Joe, we've seen something different about your marriage. We don't know what it is, but we'd like to have it, too." Authenticity is the key. Christ has liberated us to be genuine, and unless we come to grips with His provision, evangelism becomes a project rather than a life style of beauty. The leader is to be the ultimate model of authenticity. As such he is the premier, the ultimate model for evangelism when his reputation builds as a "lover of strangers."

QUALITIES OF LOVE THAT WORK

There are certain other qualities which are essential to effective church leadership. *Leaders must love each other*. This quality needs to be obvious. The men need to be freed to express their affection warmly and openly. Love is built by spending significant, regular time together. Board retreats should be times of personal evaluation where blind spots can be communicated in a spirit of love and acceptance. Leaders must share freely the current state of their spiritual pilgrimage. And they must be open to loving correction if needed. Love speaks the truth; love wounds its object to stimulate growth. Love desires the best for its object and is willing to pay whatever price is necessary to see it achieved. Love holds its object accountable for reaching agreed upon goals and objectives. Leaders are to be brothers and sisters in the fullest and richest sense of the word.

Leaders must exist together in unity. They are to be diligent in maintaining this oneness (Ephesians 4:3). They must be as one. Standing together, they must come across as willing to sacrifice for each other. Congregational members must sense the impossibility of pitting one against another. They cannot be bought by prestige or position. Jesus Christ is clearly the head of the church, and they owe their allegiance to Him and to each other. Satan's greatest inroads come at the point of unity.

It is my personal opinion that democracy can be dangerous in a church setting. Decision making based on majority rule can be extremely divisive. Under such a system someone always wins, and others lose. Personalities enter in, voting blocks develop, politicking is encouraged, and feelings are hurt. If Spirit-controlled men (based on 1 Timothy 3 and Titus 1) are appointed as leaders, is it not reasonable to believe that He can lead them all to the same conclusion? The principle of unanimity (unanimous decision making) encourages unity, builds relationships, and underscores our dependency on the Spirit for wisdom. It also keeps leaders from being "yes men" to their pastor. Just one negative vote stops any action of the group. When this would happen at our church we would encourage the one who voted against the majority. Stopping everything, we would usually drop to our knees in prayer, seeking the mind of Christ. Often the Lord would use this lone vote as a signpost, and we would reverse a decision. We experienced plenty of healthy diversity as we discussed issues, but trusted the Spirit to lead us to consensus. Certainly integrity must supersede unity. God would never call us to compromise our moral and ethical convictions to achieve unity. In a healthy body that should not be necessary.

The church leader must be well-versed in ecclesiology. That is, he should know the biblical teachings on the church. With pastors leaving every two or three years, the so-called "lay leaders" need to have strong biblical convictions concerning the nature and purpose of the church. They should invite a pastor to help them fulfill their vision of the church and its local ministry. Such books as *Sharpening the Focus of the Church* by Gene Getz, *A New Face for the Church* by Larry Richards, and *When All Else Fails, Read the Directions* by Bob Smith, should be required reading. They make great topics for a board retreat.

Let me close this chapter by sharing a personal prejudice. I do not feel a board should rotate members in and out every two to three years. It takes at least that long for board members to begin to develop quality relationships and to begin to understand the uniqueness of the church. Furthermore, it puts the pastor in a very dangerous position. He becomes the only self-perpetuating, "permanent" member of the board, and often becomes accountable to no one. He becomes *the* leader, and the rest of the leaders become ineffective. The job of a pastor is to lead with, not lord over. But he is the key person who can cultivate the environment in which effective leadership qualities can grow. The importance of his role is the substance of the entire chapter that follows.

Chapter 7, Notes

1. Charles B. Williams, *The New Testament in the Language of the People*. Copyright 1937 Bruce Humphries, Inc., (R) copyright 1965 Mrs. Edith S. Williams. Moody Bible Institute of Chicago. Moody Press. Used by permission.

2. Frank Accardy, *A Certain Kind of Man* (Olympia, Washington: Emmanuel Baptist Church, 1979), p. 14.

3. Rebecca Pippert, *Pizza Parlor Evangelism* (Downers Grove, Ill.: InterVarsity Press, 1976), p. 4.

Chapter 8

Evangelism and the Pastor

*A*lfred Sloan's definition of an organization as "the lengthened shadow of a man" reinforces the fact that the pastor's behavior is a key to health and renewal in a church. The local church in a large measure is "the lengthened shadow" of its pastor.

Our fourth question focuses on this vital fact. Let's review the questions up to this point.

Question One:	What kind of person do we want to deploy in the world?
Question Two:	What kind of church makes possible that kind of person?
Question Three:	What kind of leadership team makes possible that kind of church?
Question Four:	**What kind of pastor makes possible that kind of leadership team?**

The leader, whoever he may be, is always the focal point for renewal and change within an organization.

Recent research in secular organizations is now spelling out more clearly the what and why about the chief executive which makes him the key to the success of organizational development: *it's his behaviour pattern* (italics mine).[1]

The influence chain in a church looks something like this:

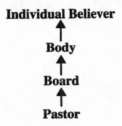

Individual Believer

↑

Body

↑

Board

↑

Pastor

Having seen his position of influence within a congregation, let's take a closer look at this person called "pastor."

WHAT SHOULD A PASTOR BE LIKE?

Napoleon once said that "a man becomes the man of his uniform." Put a military uniform on a fuzzy-cheeked kid and he becomes a different person. Unfortunately—or fortunately—we become what we visualize ourselves to be. Often that "vision" is cultural but not biblical. It is unfortunate for the church pastor when church members have predetermined what he should be like and do. Especially when their cultural convictions overpower biblical ones. The following advertisement would be funny if it weren't so true.

> WANTED: Minister for Growing Church. A real challenge for the right man! Opportunity to become better acquainted with people!
>
> Applicant must offer experience as shop worker . . . office manager . . . educator (all levels, including college) . . . artist . . . salesman . . . diplomat . . . writer . . . theologian . . . politician . . . Boy Scout lead-

er ... children's worker ... minor league
athlete ... psychologist ... vocational
counselor ... psychiatrist ... funeral director ... wedding consultant ... master
of ceremonies ... circus clown ... missionary ... social worker. Helpful but not
essential: experience as a butcher ...
baker ... cowboy ... Western Union messenger.

Must know all about problems of birth,
marriage, and death; also conversant
with latest theories and practices in
areas like pediatrics, economics, and nu-
clear science.

Right man will hold firm views on every
topic, but is careful not to upset people
who disagree. Must be forthright but
flexible; returns criticism and back-
biting with Christian love and forgiveness. Should have outgoing, friendly dis-
position at all times. Should be captiva-
ting speaker and intent listener. Will pre-
tend he enjoys hearing women talk.

Education must be beyond Ph.D. require-
ments, but always concealed in home-
spun modesty and folksy talk. Able to
sound learned at times but most of the
time talks and acts like good-old-Joe.
Familiar with literature read by average
congregation.

Must be willing to work long hours, subject to call any time day or night, adaptable to sudden interruption. Will spend at
least 25 hours preparing sermon. Additional 10 hours reading books and magazines.

Applicant's wife must be both stunning
and plain, smartly attired but conservative in appearance, gracious and able to
get along with everyone, especially
women. Must be willing to work in

church kitchen, teach Sunday school, babysit, run multilith machine, wait table, never listen to gossip, never become discouraged.

Applicant's children must be exemplary in conduct and character; well-behaved, yet basically no different from other children; decently dressed.

Opportunity for applicant to live close to work. Furnished home provided; open-door hospitality enforced. Must be ever mindful the house does not belong to him.

Directly responsible for views and conduct to all church members and visitors, not confined to direction or support from any one person. Salary not commensurate with experience or need; no overtime pay. All replies kept confidential. Anyone applying will undergo full investigation to determine sanity.[2]

Although obviously overstated, the fictitious ad reveals many cultural and biblical role expectations that the pastor must deal with and attempt to balance. The role expectations of people can be a difficult burden. The pastor who attempts to live up to all such expectations risks his health, testimony, and effectiveness.

The following is a list of common expectations for the pastor. You determine whether the expectations are cultural or biblical. Not all of the statements will be easily categorized!

Cultural	Biblical	
☐	☐	A pastor should have a personal faith in Christ.
☐	☐	A pastor should live in a parsonage.
☐	☐	A pastor should be married
☐	☐	A pastor should not have his own friends.
☐	☐	A pastor should not be paid well. (This one may fool you.)

☐ ☐ A pastor should expect his wife to be a regular church worker

☐ ☐ A pastor's job is to do the work of the ministry.

☐ ☐ A pastor's home circle should be an open circle.

☐ ☐ A pastor's children should be models for the congregation.

☐ ☐ A pastor should lead in prayer each Sunday morning.

☐ ☐ A pastor should have no obvious deficiencies or inadequacies.

☐ ☐ A pastor should have a passion for the lost.

☐ ☐ A pastor should not be accountable to his board.

☐ ☐ Only an ordained minister should preach or teach.

☐ ☐ A pastor should not reveal his needs.

☐ ☐ A pastor should avoid association with non-Christian people and enterprises.

☐ ☐ A pastor is expected to be competent in all areas of life and ministry.

☐ ☐ A pastor is public property, and therefore should be available to one and all.

And so it goes. The pressures of conformity are real; sometimes they are helpful, but often they are devastating.

What kind of pastor does it take to deploy into the world an Acts 2 Christian who is vibrant and alive for Jesus Christ? Ideally, it takes one who personifies all that we have said up to this point about our Acts 2 Christian, his local fellowship, and its leaders. Is it any wonder that James says "Not many of you should presume to be teachers . . ." (James 3:1). It was his half brother who said "everyone who is fully trained will be *like* his teacher" (Luke 6:40). The challenge is obvious.

Certainly we would expect the pastor, the ultimate behavioral model, to have the qualities of 1 Timothy 3 and Titus 1. These qualities are a destination towards which the leader progresses. No one possesses them perfectly. The pastor certainly should have demonstrated that his life is moving consistently or persistently in the development and cultivation of these qualities. We could disqualify most pastors if we took any one of the qualities and pressed hard enough for its mature and effective presence. How many would pass the test of being a "lover of strangers?" What about "managing his own family well (beautifully)"? We should not expect perfection. A pastor is simply another sinner saved by grace who is being progressively conformed to the image of Christ just like every other believer. We do not have a third category of beings. We have lost sinners and sinners saved by grace. Period.

WHAT A PASTOR IS REALLY LIKE

Most of you reading this book are not pastors. Having had seven wonderful years in the pastorate, let me share with you some personal observations about what pastors are really like. Obviously, not every characteristic fits every pastor. Having spoken to hundreds of pastors in various conferences and seminars and listened to them as they shared their hearts, I know something of what makes them tick. You may be surprised by their genuine humanness and needs.

By and large pastors are wonderful people. They really do want to help you. In fact, they often agonize over you, desiring to see Christ formed in you.

A large percentage of pastors are discouraged and in many cases defeated. Usually they won't show it, but it's there. Working with a volunteer staff and Sunday Christians is tough. Believers' lack of commitment to Christ and His purposes crushes many of them. Scores leave the pastorate every month because their dream of shepherding a flock of God's people towards maturity turned into a nightmare.

Most pastors feel extremely inadequate. Behind their Sunday morning face is one wracked by anxiety and uncertainty. In most cases their seminary training did not prepare them to deal with personal and organizational problems. At best they are skillful in one or two of at least a half dozen necessary skills and abilities. Yet churches expect them to cover all of the bases, all at once.

Many pastors are prisoners of other people's expectations. They try desperately to project "authenticity" in every area of life and ministry. To do this they must continually cover their inauthenticity. Tragically, many feel they should cover it. It is very difficult for pastors to cope with their humanity. They need help in being human, in enjoying life, in relating comfortably and naturally to Christians and non-Christians.

Pastors are often very lonely. Any leadership position is lonely, but the pastorate can be doubly so. The very word "pastor" presupposes one who leads, who commands, who knows and is in charge in every situation. He's a great guy to be around when the world's caving in, but when the fish are biting he's usually passed over as a fishing buddy, as though he couldn't be one. Many a pastor would love to be included in a fishing trip, but they are seldom invited.

By virtue of his position a pastor is often accountable to no one. Certainly there is some legal accountability established in most constitutions, but that's not what I'm referring to. Few pastors have a "pastor" (layman or otherwise) who serves as their priest and confidant. No one holds them accountable in areas of spiritual growth, family relations, and ministry responsibilities.

The pastorate can be a very attractive haven for lazy people. While at Dallas Seminary I heard Dr. J. Vernon McGee state that laziness was the number one sin of pastors. I have never forgotten his words. Businessmen have schedules to meet and quotas to produce. Regular evaluations are scheduled and completed. Performance feedback is readily available. The nature of the pastoral ministry is such that accountability is rare and difficult. How do you measure spirituality? Without some type of accountability a pastor can put in as much as a sixty-hour week and still be lazy or ineffective. Some spend many hours doing unproductive things. Others are "efficient" but not effective. In many cases the pastor can use help in time management and principles of organization and administration. The other extreme, of course, is the pastor who has a need to "burn himself out" for Jesus . . . usually sacrificing his home life for ministry.

Pastors' wives are often hurting—silently. They are literally the "walking wounded." Many of the books on being a pastor's wife should be burned. Let them be themselves, have their own friends, stay home from church if they feel like it, and never get involved in the ministry of the "church gathered" if their gifts are elsewhere. Let their children be children. Let them spill their milk, kick up their heels, or try their wings like any other red-blooded young person. If necessary, sell the parsonage and let them live like real people in a real world.

Many pastors are underpaid. As a general rule, a pastor should make as a minimum what the average person in his congregation does. He should live like his parishioners, eat like them, dress like them, drive a car like them, have a home comparable to them, and have a retirement plan like them. His salary should not be a weapon to control or manipulate him. It should be freely and graciously given with no strings attached. Certainly "God will provide," and the pastor is to "live by faith," but how about spreading the "faith" around a little bit? The pastor isn't the only one who is to "live by faith!"

The freedom to express love is denied to many pastors. They may feel it, but often cultural conditioning and faulty seminary instruction have rendered them incapable of communicating it. Start a revolution. If your pastor is this way, get a bunch of your people involved in a plot to solve the problem. Each Sunday for eight weeks walk up to him at the end of the service and give him a big hug. Tell him you love him. He'll never be the same again!

Many pastors struggle with their devotional life. For some it's almost nonexistent. Some have abandoned prayer because of repeated discouragement. Others have allowed sermon preparation to become a substitute for time with the Lord in personal devotions. They often feel guilty about this. They need your understanding and prayer.

Few pastors have any non-Christian friends. In most cases they are not reaching their neighborhoods for Christ. This lack of effective contact with non-Christians colors their understanding of separation and their practice of evangelism. Many excuse their lack of neighborhood penetration because some people do find Christ as a result of their preaching and counseling ministry. Most pastors need lots of help in building bridges to their non-Christian contacts.

Sometimes pastors can become very threatened people. Other ministries threaten them. Some cannot trust laymen. Others will not take constructive criticism. I have seen pastors of some very large churches withdraw from their staff until there is no longer any significant contact. Staff members who were friends and fellow workers are abandoned. In some cases, the pastor cannot handle "success." He really believes his press clippings and the "glorifying of the worm" ceremony held at the church door at the end of the sermon.

Unless they are angry, some pastors are not happy; unless they are fighting, some feel they are not faithful.

> It discourages me when my heroes fight eternally. One could almost regret that the liberals have lost all their influence. Since it's hardly worth it to fight them because they have no power, we fight each other. There is something inherently a part of the separatist, fundamentalist that compels him to do battle all the time. If he can't find an enemy to fight he will fight a friend. In this generation, one needs the armor of Ephesians 6 to guard against the attacks of other fundamentalists.[3]

Our Lord said, "blessed are the peacemakers." A house divided against itself cannot stand, so pastors should not seek to divide His house.

Pastors by the dozens leave the ministry each year because of moral failure. Uphold them before the Lord because the temptations are very real and opportunities for transgression abound.

God has given to the church gifted men called pastors. They are to be loved, respected, encouraged, and uplifted. They are human and face all the temptations of every other human being. They have their faults, fears, and inadequacies. Allow them the freedom to succeed and to fail. Support them and challenge them. Care for them and in love confront them. Your love and support may revolutionize them and in the process change the very personality of your church.

To help determine the kind of shepherd which stimulates beauty, I'd like to move now to considering some marks of maturity for a pastor. Again, these are goals to shoot for, a direction to move. Since pupils are to become like their teachers, they are really goals for all of us.

THE MARK OF AN EXPANDING FAITH

Faith is that God-given ability to take the promises of God out of mothballs and apply them to the challenges of everyday living. Men of faith dream God-sized dreams and then move out to transform those dreams into reality. God has put no ceiling on our dreams. In fact, He is pleased when we dream. God has said that without faith, it is impossible to please Him (Hebrews 11:6). Pleasing Him is believing Him. Faith as *belief* is affirming who He is while faith as *action* is responsible behavior in the light of who He is and what He has promised. Sometimes it is behavior which overcomes overwhelming odds in a visibly victorious manner. By faith men of God "conquered kingdoms, . . . shut the mouths of lions, . . . became powerful in battle . . ." (Hebrews 11:33-34).

More often it is a tenacious behavior which triumphantly endures in the midst of intense struggle and personal loss. "Others were tortured and refused to be released, so that they might gain a better resurrection" (Hebrews 11:35).

Some accepted joyfully the seizure of their property because they knew they had a better and an eternal possession (Hebrews 10:34).

The writer goes on to say that ". . . my righteous one will live by faith. And if he shrinks back, I will not be pleased with him" (Hebrews 10:38). Faith is not shrinking back, whether one faces *opportunity* or *oppression*. The idea "shrinking back" comes from a Greek term meaning to "take down a sail." When the Spirit of God fills our sails, and we find ourselves speeding through uncharted waters, God is displeased if we take down our sails. How often we do this. We resist the momentum of God's Spirit, preferring the "safety" of the harbor. How much easier it is to lie at anchor. Unfortunately when we do, we collect barnacles on our hulls. These barnacles are contagious, and if the corporate hull of the church becomes fouled with them, God is not pleased. Where there is no vision, people perish; churches die; Christ's reputation suffers.

As we saw earlier, our Lord warned against the leaven of the Sadducees which is rationalism. Rationalism—eliminating the supernatural—becomes the great enemy of faith. When the disciples came to Jesus and suggested He send the 5,000 into the towns and villages to buy food, they were thinking as Sadducees. When they said they had only five loaves and two fish, they were thinking like Sadducees. When Phillip asked where they could buy bread for them to eat and stated that two hundred denarii worth of bread would never feed them, he was thinking like a Sadducee. The deceptive thing about the leaven of the Sadducees is its reasonableness. Rationalism is reasonable and safe. Faith often appears unreasonable and risky. It was both unreasonable and risky for Peter to attempt to walk on water. It was unreasonable for Noah to build a boat, for Abraham to expect a son, for Moses to abandon the prestige of Egypt, and for George Mueller to care for orphans (though God miraculously supplied in his English orphanage).

Faith is the quality and an ability we must all grow in if we are to please Him. Certainly we want to do that! The great faith chapter (Hebrews 11) gives us three clues for faith building.

Belief in the Invisible

First, these faith giants saw through the problems of the natural world to a supernatural Being. Behind the trauma of the physical world, they saw (by faith) another world, another realm, but most important, *an invisible being*. They saw Him who is invisible (Hebrews 11:27). The writer to the Hebrews exhorts us to do the same: ". . . let us run with perseverance the race marked out for us. Let us fix our eyes on Jesus, the author and perfecter of our faith . . ." (Hebrews 12:1-2). Our eyes must move from the waves to the master of the waves, from the storm to the Savior, from the fire to the Father.

Pastors particularly must be "looking unto Jesus." Their gaze must penetrate problems and focus on the Prince of Peace. Noah kept pounding and sawing. His vision of God was the key to his victory. He refused to take down his sail. Abraham left the familiar and went out into the unfamiliar, the new, the untested, the uncharted, because he saw that God was the architect and builder of his future (Hebrews 11:10). Cultivation of relationship with Him who is invisible is the first key for building faith. God wants our love and devotion, but He knows the difference between devotional idleness and devoted action.

Faith in What Has Been Promised

The heroes of faith not only saw Him who was invisible, but they welcomed His promises from a distance (Hebrews 11:13). This is the second factor in building faith. As we cultivate a relationship with God we are able to claim with assurance (faith) the promises which grow out of that relationship. Sarah was enabled to conceive because Abraham considered Him faithful who had promised (Hebrews 11:11). Abraham believed God was reliable. He said it; He'll do it!

Reliability is best tested through relationship. Life is the White Sands Proving Grounds for the promises of God. Our pastor must know both the *Person* of God and the *promises* of God if he is to be a man of faith. Two things hinder this process:

1. A lack of knowledge of the promises and commitments of God.

2. A lack of faith in the Person and character of God.

Men and women of faith welcome the promises of God from a distance. That is, their major expectations are in the "distance," in the future, in life beyond the veil. The writer's comment concerning the heroes of faith is instructive. "All these people were still living by faith when they died. They did not receive the things promised; they only saw them and welcomed them from a distance . . ." (Hebrews 11:13). They didn't receive what they expected, yet they went to death expecting them. Their greatest expectations lay beyond this earth, beyond the suffering of this present world. Abraham left his country and went to the land promised to him but by faith lived in it as "in a foreign country." He didn't put down roots, he didn't build a city, instead, he lived in tents, because "he was looking forward to the city with foundations, whose architect and builder is God" (Hebrews 11:10). Mark it well, friend, this hero of faith welcomed from a great distance a city beyond his days on this earth. His gaze broke through into eternity, and the reality of the eternal city changed his life, balanced his priorities, and directed his energies. Men of faith long for "a better country—a heavenly one" (Hebrews 11:16).

Moses claimed the promises of God, and turned his back on the prestige, power, and wealth of Egypt because ". . . he was looking ahead to his reward" (Hebrews 11:26). In Hebrews 10:34 we are told that persons of faith risked their lives by showing sympathy to the prisoners. They joyfully accepted the confiscation of their property knowing that they had "better and lasting possessions" (Hebrews 10:34). They will be winners, they will not be ashamed for the choices they made because God is faithful, His promises are true, and ". . . he has prepared a city for them" (Hebrews 11:16). An expanding faith must be marked by confidence in God's promises.

Living a Faith Life Style

A real winner feels the gold medal around his neck before he enters the race. So should the pastor. He should run to win, and motivate by his courageous example a multitude to run with him. The promises of God should be the fabric of his future. Faith begins with the *Person* of God, moves to His *promises,* and then to a *pattern* for living. Ours is a living faith and a faith to be lived.

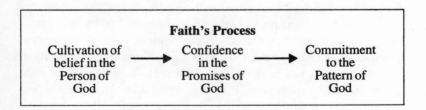

There is a faith life style. Paul said, "I want to know Christ (His Person) and the power of his resurrection (His Promises) and the fellowship of sharing in his sufferings (His Pattern), becoming like him in his death" (Philippians 3:10). The faith life style is summed up in verse 13 of Hebrews 11. "All these people were still living by faith when they died. . . . And they admitted that they were aliens and strangers on earth." Pastors of all people must make this confession. It is the Magna Charta of Christian living. These heroes of the faith abandoned any hope of ultimate fulfillment in this life. They determined to ever be foreigners in their own countries, to live as aliens in their own land.

Abraham had every right to settle down and build a city but . . . "by faith he made his home in the promised land like a stranger in a foreign country; he lived in tents, as did Isaac and Jacob, who were heirs with him of the same promise" (Hebrews 11:9). The implications of such a choice are staggering. No city on this earth, no geographical location, no second home in the mountains have foundations which will last. Therefore a regenerate being who has eternal life should abandon all hope of being satisfied and fulfilled with that which is temporal. Our heartache is eternal, and no temporal bicarbonate will ease it. Nothing less than seeing Jesus face to face and dwelling in His presence (in His city) will ever satisfy that deep longing in our hearts. It's a longing for home, and this world will never be our home.

Much of the Christian community acts as though this world was its home. Materialism is rampant. We have followed the gospel of the worldling who hopes that by doubling the cost of his new home he can double his happiness. This quest, this mission for materialism, this perverted gospel, cripples the impact of countless Christians. The visible mark of faith is an alignment with an eternal home which creates an attitude and life style marked by its contrast with the secularism of our day. This alignment refocuses everything else. It changes the Christian's goals and objectives. It redirects his gifts and abilities and resources. It redefines his mission. Suddenly eternity with Him is everything, and God's purposes in time become critical as one prepares for that great day. The self-appointed "alien and stranger" lives for the possibility of hearing his Master say, "Well done, thou good and faithful servant." Like Moses, he looks forward to the reward.

Pastors, the behavioral models of the church, must be examples of total stewardship. They should "richly enjoy" all that God has given, *but their heavenly citizenship should be obvious*. The deceitfulness of wealth, of any treasure but God Himself, is a dangerous time bomb. Some pastors err in the other direction. They parade their poverty, and continually let their "needs" be known, and then "praise God" for His wonderful provision. Be careful, and pray for balance.

Faith is the essential ingredient which pleases God. Faith is fueled as the pastor cultivates the presence of God. As D. L. Moody used to say, "I am a leaky vessel, and I need to keep under the tap." Faith is freed as the pastor develops confidence in the promises of God. It is properly focused as he adopts God's pattern of living. The man of faith is an alien sent by God as an agent of reconciliation. An ad in a secular magazine stated, "Once you discover you can change the world you'll never be the same." How true! Faith moves mountains!

The Marks of a Positive Ministry

Faith and hope are inseparable friends. The gospel itself is literally "good news." A minister should both be and communicate good news. It's largely a matter of attitude. I find that many pastors gravitate towards a negative, critical, condemning mode of life and ministry. "Some Christians are like mannequins; they don't dance, drink, or smoke. But neither does the dummy; it doesn't do anything! The witnessing life is not merely emptied of questionable or sinful things; it is filled with love, joy, peace, and long suffering characteristic of God."[4] Unfortunately some whole denominations thrive on emphasizing just the negative. I do not believe such a pattern of life and ministry is from God.

It is often thought that the Christian faith is a deprivation of joy in living, or that it is a mere pattern of religious observances, or that it is a hairsplitting system of beliefs. Christianity does involve some of these elements but they are only incidental. The modern evangelist has to sell the biblical point of view that the Christian faith is God's way to undreamed of personal fulfillment. This will necessitate a shift to a more positive point of view in order to change this false but popular image of Christianity.[5]

Pastors need to be ministers of hope. It should permeate their lives and especially their preaching ministry. "But the wisdom that comes from heaven is first of all pure; then peace loving, considerate, submissive, full of mercy and good fruit, impartial and sincere (James 3:17). We are not to beat the sheep; we are to feed them, to love them, to sacrifice ourselves for them. I believe criticism is often a substitute, a cover for poor performance.

Peter reminds us that we are to be ready to give an answer to everyone who asks us the reason for the *hope* that is within us (1 Peter 3:15). He tells us in the next verse to communicate that hope with "gentleness and respect." This positive spiritual attitude is not "pumping sunshine." Ministry is tough. It involves heartache, tragedy, and despair. Yet the shepherd needs to have a faith which produces a hope that encourages, comforts, and strengthens even as the dark clouds gather. Those who worship Jesus Christ have reason for hope. A ministry founded on and giving rise to hope is composed of several positive factors which we will now examine.

An Unveiled Face—Authenticity

One of the joys of the new covenant is that the veils can come off. Moses came down from the mountain and veiled his face so that his people could not see his glory fade away. In 2 Corinthians 3:12-18 Paul tells us that we no longer have to function as did Moses. When one "turns to the Lord, the veil is taken away" (2 Corinthians 3:16). Let's not bring back what God has taken away. The Christian pilgrimage is not one "sanctifying" experience after which we put on the veil. We don't reach a particular point at which a veil becomes necessary. The longer we walk with Him, the less a veil should be needed. Paul encourages us to look at Him with unveiled face as we "are being transformed into his likeness with ever-increasing glory . . ." (2 Corinthians 3:18).

People are attracted to authenticity. The pastor must guard himself against accepting the illusions, fantasies, or distorted expectations of his congregation. Compromise is not the issue. Integrity is the critical element. It is so easy to deceive from the pulpit, to preach about things we have not experienced and do not consistently practice. It is so easy to overstate, to play on guilt, and to imply that we have solved the particular problem long ago. If we haven't and we imply (often by what we don't say) that we have solved this problem, or no longer struggle with it, we are veiled —inauthentic.

A Diligent Student of the Word

The demands of ministry are great. But they must not take the minister away from the Book. Since when should the minister do the calling, the visitation, teach Sunday School, chair three or four committees, fold the bulletins, oversee the Sunday School and the youth ministries, plan the retreats, and on and on and on? His job has never been to *do* the work of the ministry. He is to equip *others* to do it.

Bible study, however, is very hard work. There are plenty of things to do to keep "busy" and consequently the pastor excuses his lack of preparation. Poor preaching keeps most churches poor. Poor preaching in most cases is the result of poor priorities and procrastination. The minister who is going to build a contagious congregation must handle truth skillfully, knowing that truth is the basis and foundation of beauty.

Besides direct study of Scripture, the pastor must continue to learn. Seminars, books, retreats, and significant fellowship should have high priority in his schedule. Many secular management training programs are excellent. Each local church should set aside a substantial sum for its pastor's continuing enrichment. It can be money well spent.

A Liberator of the Body

The true church is Christ in action. Whenever we allow the "church" and "Christ" to be separated in our thinking, we get into trouble. To say that "I love Christ but I can't stand my church" is really a contradiction in terms. Christ indwells both the corporate church and the individual members of it. Christ works through the church to reach the world. The marvelous doctrine of reconciliation helps us see that ultimately evangelism is what Jesus Christ is doing through His church to reach His world.

The pattern looks like this. At Christ's incarnation, God was "reconciling the world to Himself in Christ" (2 Corinthians 5:19). Since Christ ascended to His Father's right hand, the Father "has committed to us the message of reconciliation. We are *therefore* Christ's ambassadors, *as though God were making his appeal through us*" (2 Corinthians 5:19-20, italics mine). That's exactly what Christ is doing today. He entreats a lost world to be reconciled through His church, which is His body. Christ sows His good seed (beautiful seed) in the world. The world is where the work of Christ is to take place.

The pastor must focus his church outward, not inward. His motto should be, "When the saints, go marching OUT!" The church is not a holy huddle, it is a task force whose primary focus must always be the "fields white unto harvest. . . ." Unfortunately, bigger buildings, larger programs, and more staff dictate church mission. We must justify our large expenditures, and as a result, the basic evangelism strategy becomes herding fish towards our expensive, stained-glass trap.

Often allegiance to God is measured by one's attendance and participation in church programs. The logic goes something like this: if people love God, they should be at the church-house on Sunday morning; if they love the Bible, they shouldn't miss Sunday evening; if they love their pastor, Wednesday night is a must. This whole mentality contradicts the reality of the church as Christ Himself reaching out in service to a broken world. The church is God's family extending itself to meet needs in the name and through the establishment of Jesus Himself. Evangelism is what Jesus is *actually doing* through the preaching, the worship and fellowship, and the service of the church.

The pastor more than any other individual determines the character of the church's preaching, fellowship, worship, and service. The content, style, and priority of preaching in the church's life is critical to its health and beauty. If a church is to be a *learning center*, the pastor must make diligent preparation so that what is delivered is biblical, balanced, relevant, and liberating. The gospel is good news about redemption. It proclaims a message of deliverance and hope. Likewise, the pastor is the key to liberating the church to be *a healing communion*. Building up the body is simply moving it towards health. To move from sickness to health is to be in the healing business in the fullest sense of the word.

There is a direct correlation between the power of the church as a healing communion and its power as a harvest vehicle. Jesus came, not to be ministered unto, but to minister. He did not come to minister to the healthy (healthy people don't need doctors) but to the sick. Today Jesus *comes*, not to be ministered unto but to minister, and He does it through the giftedness of the body . . . assuming it has been set free to minister. Where there is great healing, where redemption is in progress, beauty arises from the ashes of shattered dreams on the mend and broken lives which have been healed. Again, the pastor and his image of himself and the ministry is often the bottleneck which thwarts the redemptive community from being redemptive. Likewise, he is the key to whether or not the church is free to worship and to respond as a family to the obvious presence of God in their midst. The service of the church is also conditioned by the pastor's vision (or lack of it). Liberating a congregation to be *God's* people in service can be very threatening. It often involves a total rethinking of the pastoral and leadership roles. In most cases it means seeking a lower profile and elevating the gifts and abilities of others.

Suggestions in the form of rhetorical questions are helpful here. Actually visualize Jesus Christ at work through the members of your fellowship. What would He do, where would He go, with whom would He associate, whom would He confront, how would He live, where would He worship? See Him in your nursery loving those kids, and watch Him leave Sunday morning and drive into your neighborhood. Is He ever "allowed" to enter the non-Christian homes? Follow Him throughout the week as He is incarnated in the life of your average church member. Does that church member act at all like Jesus of Nazareth? Is He loving the unlovely, ministering with compassion to the needy? Are the sinners, the tax collectors, and the prosititutes as well as the professional classes mingling with Him? Is He going into homes of lost people and dining with them? Listen as preaching takes place Sunday morning. Does it sound like Jesus preaching or a false shepherd who doesn't care for the sheep? Is the message filled with truth, suited for the occasion, appropriate to the needs, compassionate in its intent, clear as to its response? Is it Jesus speaking or a re-run of someone else's work? Is it pessimistic and condemnatory without an offer of a hope which clearly sets forth steps toward wholeness?

Jesus desires to literally explode Himself through the lives of His people and do greater works than He did while present on this earth. He wants once again to touch the *untouchables,* feed the hungry, bring light where there is darkness and life where there is death. He wants to bring hope to women at wells, deliver adulterers from their sin, cast out and overturn the tables of those who traffic in religion and invite the thirsty—*whoever* they are, *wherever* they are—to discover living water. Need I say more? In the counsels of eternity for reasons unknown God decided that for a short time He would link Himself (and in a sense limit Himself) to the frailties of His creatures. Why He has not evangelized with the hosts of heaven we do not know. The fact of the matter is that Jesus' mission today is done *through* us, His ambassadors. His impact, His mission, is linked to and in a sense limited to our obedience and vision. If we draw limits He has not drawn, He becomes limited in His outreach. If our hearts have no compassion for the lost, we neglect our commission and Christ's mission is aborted.

Who do you think God wants to use to reach your neighborhood? Is He doing it? Why not? Pastor, you are God's instrument to set people free, to encourage them, to liberate them, to give them the freedom and your blessing to mark the lost for Christ. It may mean you will have to change your own attitudes toward the unsaved. You may need to realign your understanding of separation with biblical truth. Perhaps you will have to eliminate some programs, change the thrust and tone of your preaching, focus again on the essentials, and start impacting your own neighborhood. People may need to be encouraged *not* to attend the programs and activities of the church so they can spend time with the unsaved. Your church may need, with your firm leadership, to move out into the community and serve it. Neglected widows may need help, injustice in your community may need to be confronted, programs may need to be implemented to care for the poor and needy . . . with no strings attached. You may need to brainstorm with the leadership about where Jesus would go in your community to meet needs, and then direct resources and personnel into that area through preaching, fellowship, and service. It is my belief that Christianity in action under qualified leadership is always effective evangelistically.

A Builder of Men

Men attract men, especially in a church context. A primary part of the pastor's job description is the building of men. To nudge men on towards maturity takes time and commitment. His major job description is to help others minister—not to do the work of ministry himself.

> The minister is like the foreman in a machine shop, or the coach of a team. He does not do all the work, nor does he make all the plays. (Though he is a *working* foreman and a *playing* coach!) If a man can't operate a lathe, the foreman rolls up his sleeves and shows him how. If a player can't carry out an assignment, the coach demonstrates how to make the play.[6]

Even though the pastor is a shepherd who loves the entire body, a ministry to men must have a special place in his heart. While in the pastorate I met with at least five groups of men each week. I met one on one with a dentist friend, with two other board members, with a group of twenty or thirty business men, with the entire board, and with the pastoral staff (seven men). Although the group dynamics were different, the purposes were similar. With mutual accountability we shared the Word, prayer, schedules, and relationships. Each year, at my request, the board of elders met in private session (without me) to evaluate my ministry, my marriage and family, and anything else they desired. This information, often painful, was shared in love and resulted in growth and encouragement. It also set a precedent, which was my purpose for seeking the evaluation in the first place. Recognizing the value of such an exercise, the board requested that this evaluation be extended to include each of them. I've included a sample evaluation sheet for your examination.

Board Evaluation Sheet

I. Growing in Ministry

    A.   What areas of giftedness do you see being exercised? Romans 12:3-8; 1 Corinthians 12:4-11.

    B.   What areas of giftedness need to be developed? 1 Timothy 4:14; 2 Timothy 1:6.

    C.   How has _____ equipped faithful men for ministry during the last year? 2 Timothy 2:2; Ephesians 4:11-16.

    D.   Are there hindrances to ministry that need to be removed? Hebrews 12:1,2.

II. Balanced in Priorities

    A.   How has _____ grown in communion with God? John 15:1-11.

    B.   How has _____ grown in relationship with his family? Ephesians 5:18-6:4.

    C.   How has _____ grown in relationship to the body? 1 Corinthians 13:4-7; Ephesians 4:25-32.

    D.   How has _____ grown in relationship with personal acquaintances? Colossians 4:5,6.

    E.   How has _____ demonstrated His concern for God's work around the world? Matthew 28:19,20; Acts 1:8.

    F.   How well does _____'s schedule reflect the biblical priorities of an elder? 1 Timothy 4:7; Romans 12:1,2.

III. Maturing in Character

    A.   What qualities of Christ are particularly evident in _____'s life? Galatians 5:22,23; 2 Peter 1:5-9.

    B.   What qualities of an elder need further development? 1 Timothy 3:1-7; Titus 1:5-9.

    C.   What project could best stimulate _____'s growth as an elder? Hebrews 10:24,25.

    D.   Additional comments and suggestions:

We as a board recognized our need to be a redemptive community. We structured our weekly board meetings so that the first hour focused on instruction and worship. Board members rotated the teaching assignment among themselves. I spent hours working with some of the men helping prepare them to preach and teach. What an exciting challenge to sit on the front row as one of them delivers the morning message! Men, help your pastor by being honest with him. I remember so well the evening in Dallas, Texas, when a man in my congregation said to me "Joe, you've been my pastor for two years; I'm disappointed you haven't built into my life more effectively." We were staying at a motel near Dallas Seminary where I had brought a team of laymen to minister for a week. We talked into the wee hours of the morning. It was a time of soul searching . . . and growth. You may need to pose a similar question to your pastor to nudge him into one of his most important responsibilities.

An effective pastor builds into his leaders until a critical mass is attained. This building of men establishes the base for a healthy and attractive ministry.

A basic axiom of growth is to add to the base and then expand the operation. Before a church is ready to add to its mass of members, it must increase the quality and quantity of its leadership. A wise pastor learns how to be a builder of men; then makes this challenge central to his ministry.

A Family Specialist

Focus on the family! This is God's critical institution, the matrix for character development. Target sermons regularly in this direction. Take advantage of excellent film series and printed materials which are available. People are hurting desperately in this area. Meet these needs and evangelism problems are practically solved. If your church cannot accept the wreckage of broken homes and shattered dreams, it is not a place where Jesus lives. Your church should be the greatest garbage dump in town. A place where the broken, oppressed, misplaced, abandoned, and unloved peoples can come and find a "family" where they are accepted and loved . . . as is.

"As is" people are Jesus's kind of people. The Pharisees despised them. They still do. "As is" people become great disciples, and great soul winners. Those who have been forgiven the most love the most. You'll be amazed at what God can do with garbage dump people. We become masterpieces to be displayed forever in His eternal gallery.

The effective church ministers effectively to families because it *is* a family. Pastor, you're the key. Be a loving father holding broken, dirty people close. Father the fatherless, rebuke the offenders, encourage the discouraged, rejoice with those that rejoice, and weep, weep, weep. If your heart is not broken by broken people you don't have Jesus' heart. If your heart is not compelled to go when lost men stumble in darkness, you don't have Jesus' heart. Pray that His mission will recapture the hearts of His children and their leaders.

A Careful Planner

The old adage is true: If you fail to plan, you plan to fail. A goal is a statement of faith about the future. It is simply an obedient response to biblical priorities. Visions remain visions unless goals are established as steps to the visions' realization. Aim at nothing and you'll hit it every time. It's true, what you see is what you'll get. A careful planner simply puts a foundation under his fantasy. Some years ago I put together a document which has been very influential in shaping my life. It contains my personal objectives, goals, and standards. I established objectives and goals in five areas: my spiritual life, my intellectual life, my physical life, my family life, and my ministry. Objectives became broad statements of purpose. I will take the area of my spiritual life as an example.

Suppose one objective is to be conformed to the image of Christ. That is a very broad, unmeasurable purpose. To achieve it I must establish several goals. One goal would be to maintain a regular Bible study program. Another might be to develop a significant prayer life. Reading Christian biographies could be another goal. If I meet these goals I will be well on my way towards my objective of Christ-likeness. Unfortunately, these goals are too general, and are unmeasureable. Therefore, I must establish standards which will quantify my goals and make them measureable. Here is a sample outline.

    I. Objective: To be conformed to the image of Christ.
        A. Goal: Regular Bible study program
            1. Standard: 30 minutes in Bible study
            2. Standard: 10 minutes in devotional literature
            3. Standard: Weekly reading of pertinent journals:
                a) *Christianity Today*
                b) *Eternity,* etc.

        B. Goal: Develop a significant prayer life
            1. Standard: 30 minutes per day
            2. Standard: Written requests with answers
                    recorded
            3. Standard: Daily prayer with wife and family
            4. Standard: Daily prayer with staff

        C. Goal: Read significant Christian biographies
            1. Standard: One biography per month

Such an exercise is invaluable. It is a proven fact that the less time you spend in planning the more time you will spend in work. The more you plan, the less time is spent in working. Perhaps the greatest value of planning is the effect of what is often called a "self-fulfilled prophecy." Planning plants seeds which enable visions to grow into realities. Planning is simply taxing the mind to solve the problems which keep us from a fruitful future. Not to plan is not to set in operation the incredible resources of the human mind. A resource which when linked with faith can move mountains. A man of vision plans . . . so does an effective shepherd.

The fifth and final question is one which only the pastor can answer. It is this: "What changes must take place in the life of the pastor to make him that kind of a person?" It is a critical question. Pastors need the insight and the feedback of their leaders to answer it effectively. The question cannot be answered unless it's asked. My prayer is that many pastors will take the risk . . . and ask.

Chapter 8, Notes

1. *Theology News and Notes* 19 (October 1973): 16,24.

2. William McRae, *The Dynamics of Spriritual Gifts* (Grand Rapids: Zondervan, 1976), pp. 123-24.

3. Truman Dollar, "An Era of Discontent and Discouragement," *The Baptist Bulletin*, February 1980, p. 28.

4. Leighton Ford, *Good News Is for Sharing* (Elgin, Ill.: David C. Cook, 1977), p. 106.

5. James Jauncey, *Psychology for Successful Evangelism* (Chicago: Moody Press, 1972), p. 39.

6. Leighton Ford, *The Christian Persuaders* (New York: Harper & Row, 1966), p. 49.

Part 3

Evangelism and You

Chapter 9

Your Home and Evangelistic Bible Studies

L ined up two or three deep around the bar, the noisy crowd's laughter and boisterous behavior drowned out the TV as it droned on and on about nothing. A gray-haired, distinguished-looking man elbowed his way through the teeming crowd until he reached the counter. Pounding on it with his fists he quieted the crowd. Attention gained, he blurted out, "Let's talk about Jesus Christ!" Somehow nobody wanted to talk. Sophisticated conversationalists who only moments before couldn't get a word in edgewise were hard put to get a word out. All talk ceased when Christ's name was introduced into the conversation. Tongues got tied, palms got sweaty, hearts palpitated, and faces turned crimson.

In a Sunday morning sermon I challenged the congregation to walk up to a group of strangers and invite them to talk about Jesus Christ. My friend, a bold and courageous new Christian, accepted the challenge and proved a point. The song is right: "there's just something about that name." No other name creates that universal response. It is highly unlikely that anyone would feel that sense of unrest, threat, or embarrassment if the conversation focused upon Mohammed, Buddha, or Joseph Smith.

Non-Christians are not the only ones who feel embarrassed talking about Jesus Christ. Christians do, too! Our English word "embarrassment" comes from the same root as barrier and barricade. It literally means "to place a bar (an obstruction) in." An embarrassed person has literally had a monkey wrench thrown into his emotional gears. Besides wanting to vanish, run, or hide, embarrassed people are often unable to act appropriately. They often can't think logically or act rationally. Embarrassment usually comes when events or circumstances reveal inadequacy or inappropriate behavior.

Embarrassment stops some believers from sharing because they don't yet feel perfect. Fearing that the non-Christian will spot some "flaws," they keep their distance so as not to be "hypocritical." (For some this is a legitimate concern . . . they *are* hypocritical.) Regardless of our laborious attempts to appear otherwise, the world knows we are not perfect. If we would allow them, they might be surprised to see that we are at least making progress in a positive, wholesome direction instead of "advancing progressively backwards" (T.S. Eliot) with the rest of society.

The topic of this chapter could well be described as "How to Perform Heart Surgery Without the Patient Knowing It!" Perhaps this chapter will be a challenge to some of our "embarrassed brethren." Believe it or not, your home could be the scene of divine surgery in which the cutting power of God's Word is used to penetrate spiritual scar tissue, laying bare men's hearts to the demands of a Holy God. We will talk about evangelistic Bible studies. My wife and I have had the privilege of being involved in numerous evangelistic studies under every conceivable circumstance. Dozens of people have discovered Christ as they interacted with others around God's principles found in Scripture. And we have found certain musts for the evangelistic effectiveness of these studies.

Let me first warn you, though, that there is a big difference between an *evangelistic* home Bible study and a home Bible study. The two do not mix. I am sure you know of Bible Studies where an overzealous Auntie Maude and Brother Jim plus a few other supercharged saints showed up ready to do battle. It was not long until the discussion turned from the simple "ABC's of the faith" to the eschatological implication of the ten horns of the beast of Daniel chapter seven. What started out to be an evangelistic Bible study turned into a society for protecting, preserving, and propagating pet theological hobby horses.

For your home to be a successful context for evangelism, you must adopt and implement a distinctive philosophy which will encourage the likes of Auntie Maude and Brother Jim to join another group capable of appreciating their precise theological insights. In the long run, this will profit your purposes of evangelism, as well as steer Maude and Jim to the right group.

A Proper View of Separation

In order to work with unsaved people, one must have *a healthy understanding of separation*. Separation is not maintaining a "radical difference" and avoiding "radical identification." A position between radical difference and identification must be maintained as a system of checks and balances. Biblical separation is not simply avoiding a negative (sin). The believer is to be separated *from* sin and separated *unto* God. Separation is not isolation from unredeemed mankind; rather it is separation from acts of personal sin and separation unto God.

Some churches today are similar to a department store where all the employees arrive at the prescribed time, lock the doors, and then sell merchandise to each other all day. To do any good, salt has to not only get out of the shaker, but it must come into contact with the food. Otherwise, it's useless.

A Trust in God's Word

An effective evangelistic strategy must *place confident trust in the power and authority of God's Word*. When people interact with its truths things happen . . . often unexpected things. Unbelievers find themselves at the foot of the cross and wonder how they got there.

God is not dependent upon our tactics and devices. Consequently we can leave behind our religious twang, our furrowed brow, our pointed finger, and our spiritual 4 x 4's (not to mention our string ties and Herbert Hoover collars).

How freeing and refreshing it is to bring people under the healthy teaching of the Word and leave the results to God. If we trust the convicting power of God's Spirit, our strategy can be "low pressure, long range."

A WHOLESOME ATMOSPHERE

The effective study must have a carefully cultivated atmosphere. This provides the context in which the gospel content has its greatest impact. In the first three or four sessions, atmosphere is probably more important than content. In a nutshell, we're talking about beauty again.

Create an atmosphere where the non-Christian feels at home. The evangelistic study is for nonbelievers, not believers. If believers are in the majority and insensitive to the group dynamics, they will soon drive the non-Christian away. The non-Christian needs to feel it is *his* group because he senses other people like him are present. I watched a group of thirty-five non-Christians diminish to practically zero because of the rudeness and insensitivity of some uninvited Christians who "crashed" the study. The only Christians who should be present are those who are bringing their non-Christian friends.

Even under these circumstances, it is best to set down some ground rules for Christians' attendance. Here are a few. First, the purpose of the study is evangelism. Second, the non-Christian must feel comfortable and welcome. Third, most of the discussion should involve non-Christians. As a general rule, the Christian should avoid active participation in discussion. Fourth, religious clichés should be avoided. Fifth, discussion of various churches and denominations should be avoided. Sixth, Christians should resist the temptation to "straighten out" doctrinal views of the participants which are not central to the issue of salvation. The issue is Jesus Christ, not infant baptism, total immersion, the inspiration of Scripture, pretribulationalism, or Post Toasties. Seventh, the Christian should refrain from bringing up all kinds of parallel passages. As a general rule the study should confine itself to one passage. Anyone can make significant observations on five or six verses. However, once the "resident experts" start spouting off other passages, the non-Christian realizes he is outgunned and out of place. Eighth, as a general rule, the Christian participants should avoid giving advice or sharing pious platitudes and spiritual bandaids. If they share, it should focus on their *personal experience of the truth,* not an untested list from some seminar or textbook. Ninth, the Christian must avoid the temptation to press for premature decisions. Tenth, the Christians should avoid the social "holy huddle" syndrome. Some of your best friends may be there, but your mission is to reach out in love to the non-Christian. He must be made to feel special. He is!

Create an atmosphere in which the nonbeliever feels free to participate. One way to encourage participation is to build the entire study around three to four key questions. For example, when I teach on the story of the woman at the well, I generally ask four questions. Normally I divide the group into two or three smaller groups, appoint leaders (usually non-Christians), and let them wrestle with the questions. What a thrill it is to see them interact with God's powerful Word. After twenty minutes or so, I call the groups back together and let each group share its finding. We have lots of fun in the process. You want to know what the questions are? O.K., here they are!

1) Describe the physical appearance of the woman at the well. What did she look like?

2) Describe the emotional condition of this woman (rejected by five men and living with a sixth).

3) What did Jesus offer as a solution to her problem?

4) Does His solution have any relevance to the needy people in our world? If so, how does it become operational in our experience?

The questions about her appearance spark lots of humorous discussion. To have six men, she must have been pretty attractive. On the other hand, having put up with six men. . . .

Imagine the emotional state of one who sought love, security, and affection from five husbands and struck out. A woman's number one fear is to be used and abandoned. Five times she realized her worst fear. Believe me, there will be some identification going on. The Samaritan woman has legions of contemporary brothers and sisters still trying to ease eternal heartaches with temporal bicarbonates. What an exciting time it is to hear them discuss the contemporary relevance of Christ's ancient offer of thirst-quenching water. Sometimes they almost literally lead themselves to the Lord!

Another way to encourage the participation of the non-Christian is to compliment him for his observations. We often don't know what to get excited about. It may be a vanilla, model T Ford-truth he discovers . . . one we've known since church camp days. But if it's brand new to him, GET EXCITED! Count on it, when the zest goes, the rest goes! It's a sin to bore people with God's Word. Watch the participation profile. Don't let one or two answer all the questions. Let them know you are not afraid of silence. Some people get real nervous when no one responds and feel they must talk even if they have nothing to say. If someone persists in dominating, talk to him after the session about this unfortunate pattern. Try to keep from becoming an "answer man." Often it's good to throw the question back to the group by asking, "What do some of you think?"

Another way to encourage participation is to *write down key observations* made by the group members and write their names beside their observations. When you summarize the group's conclusions at the end of the meetings, mention both the observation and the person who made it. "Susan shared the key observation about Christ's sensitivity to the woman's need for something which would satisfy her desire for security."

Participation is encouraged by an open, free, unthreatened leader. Group members may be hostile. Some are present under duress. Others may delight in asking "sticky questions." If you don't know the answer, admit it. "Hey Jim, that's a great question. Let me think about it. I'm not prepared to answer it right now. I'll bounce it off my pastor and get back with you next week."

Participation is encouraged by variety. The worst method is the same method. Discussions, tapes, films, role playing, skits, and questions and answers are but a few possible methods. Be creative! People love it.

Create an atmosphere in which the nonbeliever feels loved and accepted. Much of the previous discussion is pertinent to assuring an atmosphere of love and acceptance. In addition to the previous discussion, let me underscore some additional factors. The expectation of most non-Christians who dare to venture into anything with a "religious" label is to be judged and condemned. They often feel awkward, guilty, and ill at ease. "The unchurched person often has a built-in expectation of being rebuffed. He thinks we can smell his sin in his clothes."[1] Unfortunately, their expectations are often not unfounded. The sensitive, caring, loving Christian should therefore go out of his way to make sure the non-Christian feels welcomed and loved. If he does, he'll never recover. Group love and acceptance seems to be a basic need of the human heart. "Apparently we are driven irresistibly to come into such close relationships with groups that we become important to them and they to us."[2]

Somehow we must overcome the natural instinct to protect and hide, and demonstrate by our attitudes and actions that our friendship offers fulfillment and blessing for the non-Christian. As they feel accepted, they have "a built-in inclination to accept the group's religious beliefs even before they know them. It becomes an easy step to graduate from the social functions to the religious activities."[3]

A congenial, accepting emotional atmosphere eases communication and increases the impact of truth. The host and hostess are often the critical key to the success of the group. (1) They should have the gift of hospitality, i.e., the ability to make people feel welcome and secure. (2) They should understand the purpose and philosophy of the evangelistic study. (3) The effective host has significant non-Christian friends. (4) Effective hosts do not demand regenerate behavior from unregenerate people. (5) Effective hosts learn the names of the group members. There is no sweeter music than one's own name! (6) Effective hosts are skilled at draw-ing people into conversation. The effective host realizes the importance of tying people together into webs of friendships. (7) Effective hosts are sensitive to the needs of people at the study. Such routine things as temperature, ventilation, lighting, ash trays, and extra Bibles are on the host's mental checklist.

EXPOSURE, EXPOSURE, EXPOSURE

A final ingredient of effectiveness for evangelism in these studies comes as you continue to spend time with the group. Put in three words, it is *exposure, exposure, and exposure*. Christians in the study should make their home circle an open circle. During the course of the study, social engagements can be scheduled. The Christians need to take the initiative in setting up dinner engagements, recreational outings, and other group activities which will allow the non-Christian the opportunity to hear some of the music of the gospel. He needs to know that Christians can laugh, play, and have fun.

We have found that a potluck about four or five weeks into a study was a great way to strengthen relationships and build bridges. The group members thoroughly enjoyed setting aside an evening just for food and fellowship. Some of God's most significant work takes place around a dinner table.

Group activities build esprit de corps and tie people together. We found that a weekend retreat can be extremely effective in opening people to the gospel. There is nothing which can compare to getting away for a couple days with a mixture of sensitive Christians and searching non-Christians. It's dynamite. A word of caution: Focus on fun and fellowship. Resist the temptation to dump the whole load on your "captive audience." The key: balance, common sense, and a yieldedness to the Spirit's direction.

SUGGESTIONS FOR THE FORMAT

An evangelistic study need not be rigidly formatted. But there are some general suggestions for the planning of such a gathering. Some type of refreshments need to be planned. The informal chatting which goes on around the refreshment table performs a valuable function. It helps break down barriers. The refreshment time also provides a sounding board for personal reactions to the Bible study. Likewise, it offers an excellent opportunity to initiate conversation concerning spiritual things. Refreshments should be served at the *beginning* of the class time. Besides establishing a congenial atmosphere, it allows a "latecomer" to arrive fifteen minutes "late" and still be on time for the study itself. For example, if refreshments are served at 7:30 sharp, and the study starts right at 7:45, a couple can arrive at 7:40, enjoy a quick cup of coffee and not be late for the study. Most of the people will arrive around 7:30 so they can enjoy the time of fellowship and fun. Furthermore, refreshments are still available at the conclusion of the study for those who desire to stay longer. The hostess must resist the temptation of personally supplying the refreshments each week. Let other women volunteer. Sign them up ahead of time. It helps assure their continued presence at the study (at least the night they bring the goodies). Furthermore, it helps build the sense of it being "their group."

Utilize the phone. "You have not because you phone not" should be your motto. Personal contact goes a long way towards assuring the continued participation of group members in the study.

Make every effort to begin and end on schedule. If the study is to go until 9:00 p.m., stop at 9:00 no matter how exciting the discussion may be. It's better to leave them "longing than loathing." A good group leader knows how important it is to stop at a "high point" rather than trying to get extra "mileage" out of it.

Normally I close a study something like this. "Well, gang, it's 9 o'clock; time to quit. Some of you have baby sitters and need to get home right away. However, some of you may want to stay and continue our discussion. Let's take a five minute break. Grab a cup of coffee, and if any of you want to continue our discussion or have further questions, I'll be happy to stay and be of help." Often half the group will hang around and continue to talk through the implications of the study. These dialogues sometimes last several hours. Sometimes the most significant spiritual advances are made during these unstructured, informal bull sessions. Be especially sensitive to those who hang around and "straighten up the chairs." Often such a person wants to talk about spiritual things and doesn't know how to begin. But remember, it is important that you keep your word and end the "formal study" right on time.

Have extra Bibles available. Many never take their Bibles to church, much less to a "Bible study." They might be embarrassed to be seen with one! Suggest that next week they "dust off their Bible, wrap it in a plain brown wrapper—and bring it." They will. Once you get to know some of the non-Christians, invite different ones to read the passage under consideration.

Feel free to use humor; in fact, encourage it. Many non-Christians are delighted to discover that Christians can laugh and have a good time. Don't be afraid to laugh at yourself. By the way, use personal illustrations when they are appropriate. Don't, however, limit them to your "successes." Sometimes your failure experiences have much more educational impact. Whatever you do, don't take yourself too seriously! Relax.

Pray for each class member daily! Make a list and encourage each participating Christian to do the same. This is the real level of conflict, and, to succeed, the study must be undergirded with prayer. Normally, however, I do not begin or end the actual study with prayer. This would vary with the circumstances. It is my feeling that sometimes the non-Christian isn't ready for it.

Continuous evaluation is important to assure quality studies. If you are leading the study group, ask two or three key people to evaluate your leadership and the group's interest and response. Never assume motivation. In every group session a leader must overcome an initial inertia. This is where a good study or a personal experience shared at the beginning can "break the ice" and get the group rolling. Pay attention to how the group session ends. An effective leader summarizes the group's deliberations in such a way that the members sense that significant observations were made and significant conclusions were reached. There needs to be a sense of resolution or "closure." Otherwise, many conclude that the group simply "pooled their ignorance."

As mentioned earlier, jot down significant observations and the name of the one who contributed it during the course of the study. Use this record of observations as the basis of your summary. Not only will it reinforce the important truths, it will affirm the group members.

Finally, vary the content according to the needs of the people. The following are some suggested topics for consideration.

1. A series on the home.
2. An overview of the Bible, such as "Walk Through the Bible."
3. A series on the inspiration and the reliability of Scripture.
4. A series on evolution and the biblical view of creation.
5. A series on the Bible and modern culture.
6. A series on contemporary theology and Scripture.
7. Individual book studies: John, Mark, Romans, etc.
8. Biographical studies (Biblical characters).
9. Doctrinal studies: A series on basic Bible doctrine.
10. A series on *20 Difficult Questions:* "Are the Heathen Lost?", "Is the Bible Inspired?", etc.
11. A series centered around a significant Christian book, such as *Mere Christianity* (C.S. Lewis), *The Genesis Flood* (Morris), *Escape from Reason* (Schaeffer), *The Late Great Planet Earth* (Lindsey), *Killing Giants, Pulling Thorns* (Swindoll), *Secrets to Inner Beauty* (Aldrich).

GETTING STARTED

When inviting friends to participate in the study, don't panic. Here are some suggested "invitations." "I'm sure you are aware,

Bill, of the pressures exerted on the family today. Homes are breaking up at an unprecedented rate. Ruthe and I are concerned about these trends, and we have invited five to six couples to participate in a study of biblical principles of marriage and family life. We'd love to have you join us." Incidentally, I have found marriage and family to be one of the most valuable topics for an evangelistic study. Chuck Swindoll's book, *Strike the Original Match*, would be an excellent text to use. It has a study guide which makes it even more valuable.

If the study is going to focus on one of the books of the Bible, an invitation might sound something like this. "I know you are aware of the fact that for years the Bible has been the number one selling book in the world. No man is really educated who is not at least familiar with its basic content. We thought it would be fun to get seven to eight couples together and work through selected portions of John's gospel. The study will be informal and discussion-centered. We'd love to have you join us." After the initial introduction, one should discuss the length of the series. People are more apt to come if they know it is for only eight to ten weeks.

A series of films may be the easiest way to launch a neighborhood study. One church in Texas started twenty-six evangelistic home Bible studies by showing the Moody Science films each week for twelve weeks. Why not rent one film per week and then schedule it to be shown in a different neighborhood each night during the week. You will find that when the film series is over, the vast majority of the groups will want to continue. They have made new friends, they have been challenged intellectually and spiritually, and have tasted fellowship at a deeper level. Of course, being perceptive, you have anticipated this response and are ready to suggest that the group take another ten weeks to study John's gospel (or Romans, Marriage and Family, etc.). James Dobson's film series on the family is another powerful tool for evangelism.

Believe that people will find Christ. Expect them to respond and anticipate sharing Christ personally. Look for opportunities to talk individually with seeking people in or out of your study. I find it best to set up an appointment where we can discuss their concerns in a private setting with no fear of interruption.

Make your home circle an open circle whether or not you actually have a "formal study." Believe me, if they become your friends, they already are predisposed to become a friend of Christ.

Isn't that what evangelism is all about? Living beautifully and opening up our webs of relationships so that others can see His beauty . . . in us!

Chapter 9, Notes

1. Leighton Ford, *The Christian Persuaders* (New York: Harper & Row, 1966), p. 70.

2. James Jauncey, *Psychology for Successful Evangelism* (Chicago: Moody Press, 1972), p. 56.

3. Ibid., p. 60.

Chapter 10

Your Nonbelieving Neighbor

S o, how do you reach your neighbor? Let's assume that you really want to be a neighbor to someone spiritually. You desire to develop the "capacity to draw near." Following are some keys to developing redemptive relationships. It should be noted that they are not necessarily in a logical or chronological order. It is very likely that you will be involved with two or three of these key elements at the same time. These keys are simply guidelines or stepping stones to help you become an effective member of the "second incarnation." What's the first step?

VISUALIZE THE NEIGHBORHOOD READINESS FOR CHRIST

Visualize the Spirit of God hovering over your neighborhood. This is the first key. When I go fishing, birds are often the key to locating fish. Gulls will frequently circle in a particular spot because feeding fish are driving the small minnows (their dinner) to the surface. Gulls join the feeding frenzy and inadvertently tip off the perceptive fisherman where to fish for his dinner.

In a very real sense, the effective evangelist believes God's Spirit will lead him to the schooling fish. No one wants to be involved in a losing proposition. Many budding fishers of men are defeated before they get a line in the water because they are convinced no one is interested, seeking, or already prepared by God. Our Lord has already told us the fields are white unto harvest. Believe me there are Spirit-prepared people living in close proximity to you who are seeking answers. God will lead you to these people like the birds lead fishermen to fish—if you're looking.

For many, the first step in neighborhood evangelism is attitudinal. If they think they will be successful or unsuccessful, they're right. What we anticipate in life is usually what we get. If you say, "I can't do it," you're probably right, especially if you firmly believe you can't. God says you can. Who do you intend to believe? Actually, this principle is a very practical one which shapes your whole attitude and approach to being a neighbor.

I'm a jogger, and as I run through my neighborhood, I see more than just houses, garages, and automobiles. Those houses have people with names and faces living in them. Those I know by name I remember by name. As I regularly visualize the Spirit of God hovering over my neighborhood, I am encouraged to be about the King's business. It's true, where there is no vision, people (your neighbors) perish. Obviously, not every neighbor is ready or responsive.

Remember the pattern however. Witness begins with *presence,* moves to *proclamation,* and then on to *persuasion.* For some, the extent of your evangelistic mission may be to simply expose them to a healthy presence—the music of the gospel. Hopefully, God will use you to bring some of your neighbors to the point of a verbal explanation of the good news (the words of the gospel). The last chapter will focus on how to present the words.

When you have cultivated a friendship and become aware of some of your friend's needs, your gospel presentation becomes much more powerful because it becomes a potential solution to both his real and felt needs. When a friendship has been established, it is much easier to sense the appropriate time for moving from presence to proclamation and persuasion. Often our attempts to "persuade" are premature because we really don't know whether the individual is in a "sowing, watering, or harvest" condition.

Make an Initial Acquaintance

God knows the responsive hearts in your sphere of influence. How do you locate them? Social relationships are the key to finding the Spirit-prepared, schooling fish.

This, then, is the second key: *Those people who respond to you socially are the schooling fish*. To carry the fishing analogy (not without biblical precedent) a step further, your divine fish locator is social relationships. As you begin to relate to your neighbors, some will respond to you and some won't. Again, it is important that you seek the Lord's help in building towards genuine friendships. It shouldn't be a relationship with a hook. Those who respond to you are great candidates for discovering Christ.

I have seen this principle affirmed over and over again. One day I spent forty-five minutes with a neighbor discussing the essence of the gospel. He initiated the conversation, and as we sat watching the surf at the Oregon coast, I shared some foundational principles of the gospel. The conversation was both casual and deeply significant. This moment came after months of friendship. Both families spent the morning together playing on the beach. We consider them to be good friends. We enjoy their company. After talking about spiritual things, we shifted the conversation to the possibility of some fishing trips this fall.

A model from the world of real estate becomes instructive at this point. A real estate firm in Salem, Oregon, assigns its agents to a 500 family "farm." They are expected to contact every family once per month for a year. The contact may be a personal one, a telephone call, or a letter. Research indicates that it takes at least six contacts for people to remember who the agent is and whom he represents. During this time of "building relationships," the agents are encouraged *not* to go in the house (good psychology, every one else is trying to get their foot in the door). Furthermore, they are encouraged *not* to ask for a listing during this "get acquainted" time. Obviously there would be exceptions to these restrictions, but they do illustrate an understanding of what it takes to create a favorable climate for selling real estate.

After the initial year of regular contacts, the agent continues to communicate with his "farm members" on a scheduled, systematic basis. Research indicates that if this pattern is followed consistently for one year and a half, the agent will get eighty percent of the listings.

What do they know that we either don't know or overlook?

First, people do not like to be confronted by strangers seeking entrance into their homes. In fact, in many communities this is a social faux pas. The salesman or any other unknown professional who arrives at the door is automatically confronted with a high sales resistance. If the door is opened, the homemaker does it with a determination not to be "taken in" by sales talk. The salesman professionally represents his goods, and consequently his sales pitch must be discounted at least fifty percent. However, if a friend comes over and shares a glowing personal testimony of the value of the salesman's product, the reaction is apt to be markedly different. A satisfied customer is the most effective sales person.

Second, people are more inclined to do business with acquaintances than strangers. Third, it takes time and effort to build a healthy decision-making climate. Fourth, there is no substitute for time. Sometimes it is necessary to "make haste slowly."

Your goal is to build a climate for effective decision making. We've lived at our present location for over two years and are just beginning to see people respond. With great anticipation we wait for the harvest. We are surrounded by schooling fish. So are you.

Obviously, you cannot adopt a 500 family farm, but how about a 5 to 10 family farm. By extending your friendship to the neighborhood at large, you will discover 3 to 4 families who seem to be responsive. Block parties, Christmas open houses, and other neighborhood activities provide opportunities for exposure.

ESTABLISH A GROWING RELATIONSHIP

A third key follows close on the heels of the second: *To discover schooling fish, you must get acquainted.* Ask God to give you help in how to get to know your neighbors. Get to know their names. Be certain you pronounce them correctly. Second, smile!

Be the kind of family your neighbors would want to know. If you want to build redemptive friendships, be friendly! Third, be a good listener. Discover and discuss his interests rather than your own. I find that many Christians get tongue-tied when it comes to conversation with non-Christians.

Sometimes it's helpful if you have some subject categories in mind. For example:

Profession or career

Hobbies

Sports and recreation

Family activities and interests

Vacations

Children's activities and accomplishments

Current news items

Personal properties: boat, cars, pets, gardens, etc.

Religious background

Current projects and home improvements

Current books, films, etc.

Fourth, take the initiative to be of help when it is appropriate. If he's painting his house, grab a brush! Offer to mow the lawn and look after the house and pets while they're on vacation. Do they need a baby sitter? Sit for them. Take their children on a picnic with yours.

EXTEND AN INVITATION TO YOUR HOME

A fourth key is *to invite them to your home*. Your goal is to advance your back fence relationship towards a more significant friendship. Meals are a great way to do it. As a general rule, it is good to have a definite reason for inviting them. It may be simply to enjoy your new barbecue recipe or share some homemade ice cream. They might enjoy seeing slides of your vacation trip (notice I said they "might").

Don't be too elaborate if you entertain them for dinner. A formal dinner with crystal, china, and sterling silver isn't necessary. They would probably feel more relaxed and "at home" with a good barbequed hamburger and a coke. If your meal is too "elaborate" you are less likely to be invited to their home because the wife may not be able to match your "production." This does not mean the meal cannot be prepared and served in a lovely, gracious manner. It should be!

But what if you feel awkward about entertaining non-Christians? You feel socially inept? Let me suggest that you find someone in your church who really has the gift of hospitality and invite them *and* your neighbor over for dinner. Blend their gift with your concern and you've got a winning combination! Explain your dilemma to them and let them help you ease through. Their warmth and social skills can be the catalyst to weld the bond of friendship between you and your neighbor. Believe me, it works!

Sometimes as a gesture of friendship, your neighbor may bring over a bottle of wine. This is a common and accepted social grace in the non-Christian community. Don't panic. A judging, "self-righteous" attitude is not necessary (or biblical). You have three options. First, if you are not free before the Lord to participate (as with any doubtful thing), you may thank them for their thoughtfulness and graciously decline, returning it to them. Second, you can graciously decline but offer to serve them. Many feel free before the Lord to do this. Third, if your conscience has liberty in this area, you may thank them and participate if you desire. Whatever else may be said, the sin is not participation (assuming freedom of conscience); it is intoxication. Within the Christian community around the world, I have observed mature, Spirit-led, knowledgeable Christians exercise each of the options.

Contrary to the opinion of some Christians, no one option is more "spiritual" than another. I am not advocating or encouraging anyone to adopt any particular position. That is between the individual and His Lord. Having non-Christians around regularly, I know that this issue will come up. Regardless of your personal position, if you are going to be with non-Christians, be prepared to respond to this type of situation in a loving, sensitive manner.

When your neighbors are over for dinner, don't feel compelled to "say" something spiritual. Many seem to feel that if they have not shared their "witness" before the evening is over, they have failed. Not so. One couple we saw trust Christ took three years of careful cultivation. For most of that period, spiritual things were off limits. It soon became obvious we were not free to discuss such matters. During this time we probably ate together at least thirty times. I wish you could meet this couple today! Patience does pay off.

I would suggest that you have grace at the meal. It is your home, and it is natural for you to do this. Don't preach or share a quickie "witness" during the prayer. Be brief, and thank the Lord for your neighbors by name. I usually do not lead in prayer when we are at a restaurant with non-Christians. This can be an embarrassing experience for them.

CULTIVATE COMMON INTERESTS

Let me share a fifth key: *Do things together*. The goal is to build a reservoir of common, shared experiences. As your backyard fence relationship develops, discover what interests them. Sometimes it's good to think through a list of possible common ground "contact points." Put a check by those which would be options for you as you think about specific neighbors and their interests.

Tennis	Hunting	Service Clubs
Golf	Skiing	Garden Clubs
Fishing	Cycling	Coffee
Sewing	Jogging	Flying
Boating	Scouting	Gardening
Model Trains,	P.T.A.	Woodworking
planes, etc.	Investments	Playing Bridge
Bowling	Sports Events	Cooking Classes
Indian Guides	Rodeos	Gourmet Clubs
Movies	Recreational	Volunteer
Concerts	Vehicles	Activities
Lunch	Guns	Stitchery
Ice Skating	Eating	Quilt Making
Rafting	Knitting	Hiking
Racquet Ball		

Certainly there are items in this list which both you and your neighbor enjoy in common. It is important to discover these contact points and use them as relational building blocks. You probably have a number of common interests. As I sit here in my study writing, my wife is out with a neighbor gal going through some model homes. They both share an interest in interior design.

When you are in your neighbor's home, look for clues to his/her interests. A shop full of woodworking tools, a well-stocked sewing room, or basement shelves full of home canned fruits can be excellent conversation starters/contact points. Seasonal events such as fairs, rodeos, and ball games have built-in opportunities for friendship cultivation.

On two occasions Ruthe and I have been involved in block parties which involved as many as seventy-five people. The police were quite willing to block off the street for us. This done, we borrowed tables and chairs from the church and set them up for serving and eating. Volleyball nets strung across the street provided an outlet for the athletically inclined. Contests and prizes for the kids proved to be popular. We had a bike decorating contest which the kids enjoyed, not to mention egg tossing, sack races, etc. Six barbeques were rounded up for cooking hamburgers. Cranking the homemade ice cream freezer added to the fun and fellowship.

Block parties are super for providing a quick exposure to the majority of your "family farm." It enables you to look for responsive people who may be candidates for the "good news." If for no other reason, they are worth doing just for the fun and fellowship.

Make Holidays Count

A sixth key: *Capitalize on the holiday seasons*. Christmas, New Years, Labor Day, and Thanksgiving provide great opportunities for extending and enriching relationships within your "family farm." Why not plan the greatest Christmas Open House on your block! Pack them in, serve some super refreshments, sing carols together, and then let different neighbors share the most memorable events of past Christmases. There is no need for a "devotional" or "gospel witness" to make the evening a success. Last Christmas we went to a neighborhood caroling party with about fifty neighbors. In the fall we borrowed a cider press and invited some neighbors over to make cider and eat hot doughnuts.

Be sensitive to widows, widowers, one-parent families, and those who are alone during the holidays. Since moving to Portland, we've had the joy of sharing our holiday season with a widower who is eighty years old. At this point he doesn't know the Lord, but our family prays for him, and believes God is going to touch his heart. The last time I took him to lunch, I got him started talking about the old steam-driven threshing machines of another era. As he answered my dozens of questions, he literally lit up and glowed. He knew all about how they worked, and it brought back happy memories to relive some of his childhood years. I was thoroughly fascinated with the conversation. When we last had him over for dinner, he held me and my son Stephen spellbound for nearly an hour as he shared his knowledge and experience of working in mines. Soon I intend to share the simple plan of salvation. We believe he has heard the music of the gospel as he shared our "hearth and home" on numerous occasions. We love him and believe that he knows it.

Capitalize on holidays. They're great times to show your love in special ways. Hearts are often more receptive during these special times of the year!

BE AVAILABLE FOR THE HURTING

A seventh key is more urgent in nature: *Be available to help when people hurt*. In other words, look for wounded fish. Life is tough. Sickness, death of a loved one, marital problems, financial reversals, and other pressures provide opportunities for the Christian to express Christ's love through serving and caring for members of his "farm family." Remember, people don't care how much (or what) you know until they know how much you care! The hurts of others are your opportunities to become good news to them. I believe those opportunities are often arranged by God Himself. A helping hand and a sympathetic, listening spirit give your beliefs validity and impact. Mowing lawns, taking over meals, babysitting, shopping, and driving are some ways to help people in need.

One caution: Don't forget . . . you have needs. How about letting others meet some of them. Maybe the greatest gift you can share is the gift of your need. When conversations focus on some of the normal marriage and family problems, remember that you have some, too. Don't act as if you don't or you'll come across unauthentic.

In relational evangelism, availability is often the greatest ability. Be a listening, sensitive, giving, caring Christian friend and look out . . . it's contagious.

BECOME A GIVER OF BOOKS

An eighth key is an easy one to adopt and apply: *Give them something to read or listen to*. Be casual about it. Put some good Christian literature on your coffee table. Be sure they are top quality. Chuck Swindoll's *Killing Giants, Pulling Thorns* is a great example. Hal Lindsey's *The Late Great Planet Earth* is another powerful book. Stick with books which are need-centered and have good graphics. Often they will pick up a book and start thumbing through it. If they express an interest, give it to them, or drop by later with another. Have some on hand which you can give them. "Hey, Bill, this is a super book. I'd love you to read it and tell me what you think of it."

If they are struggling with family concerns, there are many good books available to help them. If they have a philosophical bent, C.S. Lewis's *Mere Christianity* is a good book to give them. Check with your local Christian bookstore for other selections suitable for a non-Christian. Whatever you do, be sure they are quality books. Don't be cheap! Sometimes a good modern translation New Testament makes a good gift.

There are some very challenging tape series which are effective in evangelism. Be sure, however, that you listen to the tape first! It should be positive in tone and attitude (after all, the gospel is *good news*), need-centered, and biblically sound. A good "evangelistic" tape doesn't necessarily have to deal with the subject of evangelism. Tapes on marriage and family relations, prophecy, Christian evidences (apologetics), and well-presented personal testimonies can be powerful evangelistic tools.

Christian magazines certainly should not be overlooked. Parents struggling with teen-agers might be delighted to know about *Campus Life* magazine. *Moody Monthly, Christian Life, Eternity,* and *Virtue* are but a few of the fine magazines available. Calling attention to a particular article and then giving them the magazine often is a good way to expose them to the gospel. I would suggest that you generally avoid the bumper sticker, wall plaque mentality. At least be sure they are tasteful, accurate, and of good quality.

Be creative in your use of Christian resources. Purchase a supply of quality items and keep them readily available. Consider such expenditures part of your tithe (even if you don't get a tax receipt). Remember, it was God who said that "he that winneth souls is wise." In all of these activities, your goal is to become a servant to your neighbor.

FIND AN APPROPRIATE HARVEST VEHICLE

A ninth key: *Look for an appropriate harvest vehicle.* Whether you use a lure, a worm, a hook, or a net, fish can be caught in numerous ways! Select the proper bait, however. One doesn't use trout flies for yellow tail. Live squid get their attention and make excellent bait.

Once while fishing in Mexican waters for yellow tail, we hit a school of them and boated 131 in a little over an hour. We were using live squid, but that wasn't all that kept the fish coming back. As soon as we hooked up, the deck hands started chumming the water with chopped minnows. In a very real sense, we "chum" the spiritual waters as we function as salt and light. In a practical sense we do this by spending time with our non-Christian friends, discovering their interests, sharing their fellowship, and bearing their concerns. But a time comes when it is appropriate to pray towards involving them in some type of ministry vehicle. A sensitivity towards their preferences and personal views is important. For a nonathletic vegetarian, an invitation to hear an all pro athlete at a steak fry probably is not appropriate or in good taste. If there must be an offense, let it be the offense of the gospel, not the manner in which the gospel is presented (whether verbally or non-verbally).

There are numerous "harvest vehicles." Here are some examples:

> Evangelistic Dinners
> Home Bible Studies
> Businessmen's Breakfasts
> Mayor's Prayer Breakfasts
> Christian Movies
> Conferences or Retreats (Forest Home, Mt. Hermon, etc.)
> Seminars (Bill Gothard, Leadership Dynamics, etc.)
> Fishing/Hunting Trips
> Church Sports Program
> Special Concerts (Bill Gaither, Evie, Church Musicals, etc.)
> Church Sponsored Craft Classes (Pottery, Carpentry,
>   Painting, Stitchery, Knitting, Photography, etc.)
> Church Sponsored Neighborhood Teas
> Boys Brigade/Indian Guides, Indian Princesses, etc.

Obviously, the list is limited only by man's creativity. Skim the list again and note how many of these activities are suitable for blending Christians and non-Christians together. Imagine what could happen if a church member with oil painting ability was asked to teach a church-sponsored class open to the general public. A well-equipped shop could be a great vehicle for bringing people together in relationships with great redemptive potential.

A fishing club centered around a mature Christian who knows fishing inside and out would be a very attractive vehicle to involve your neighbor in if he loves fishing. I've been part of such groups. There is lots of time for getting close to needy people on a fishing trip!

Mariners Church in Newport Beach, California, started because a group of businessmen became burdened for their community. With no intention of planting a church, they started a Christian Leadership Week. The Junior Chamber of Commerce sponsors it. No clergy are involved in its planning or execution. It is totally lay-led and as a result has been very effective. Liberal pastors who want to get in on the action are invited to send a layman to get involved. Somehow they can't seem to get their laymen interested in evangelism.

Each morning businessmen's breakfasts are held in several country clubs in the area. No ministers are allowed to speak. (This keeps it a city-wide event, free from the pressures of the local council of churches.) Two local business people (after careful preparation) speak at each breakfast. The messages are short and to the point. Speakers are asked to avoid references to specific churches, creeds, or controversial religious issues. The central topic is the gospel and how it has been personalized in their own experience. The women sponsor teas at which they share their testimonies. Evenings are filled with home meetings at which laymen share.

A Mayor's Prayer Breakfast climaxes the week. As many as 2,000 attend this function. The same morning, 500 to 600 high schoolers pack out a similar breakfast designed just for them. Usually a well known athlete or public figure speaks at this gathering. Service clubs, cooperating with the Christian Leadership Week, often have speakers at their meetings. One week we had 102 speakers. Dozens are influenced each year by this strategic event. Several of our board members found Christ through the activities of the "harvest vehicle." The church that I pastored is one of the fruits of this original vision. Christian Leadership Week was designed to provide an opportunity for Christians to invite their non-Christian friends.

A church which takes evangelism seriously should schedule several yearly events, classes, or activities which are appropriate harvest vehicles. The church newspaper should not only publicize these events but also other functions scheduled in the broader Christian community.

These harvest vehicles (check the list again) are necessary because most non-Christians avoid the big step from where they are to a Sunday morning church service. To bring your neighbor to a point of decision may involve inviting him to participate in three or four "harvest vehicles." Some will obviously be more frontal or direct in their presentation of the gospel than others. It is the cumulative impact which is important. (It should be said that neighbors may come to Christ without direct involvement in any type of "harvest vehicle.") My wife and I found evangelistic Bible studies like those described in the previous chapter to be an especially effective vehicle.

PLANT SEEDS FOR SALVATION

Your friendship may progress to the point where nonbelieving friends virtually ask you how to become a Christian. This is not uncommon, especially if you have been a good "seed planter." This is the tenth key: *Be a good "seed planter."*

There will be opportunities during your friendship to communicate bits and pieces of both the gospel itself and your own personal testimony. We already discussed the role of books and tapes in this pre-evangelism process. The temptation is to unload the entire evangelistic dump truck the first time the conversation turns to spiritual things. As a general rule, this is not a healthy pattern to follow. Gradually directing a person to Christ through seed planting is a much preferred approach.

First, discuss his religious background. "Jim, we've never had a chance to chat about your own religious background. At what point are you in your own spiritual pilgrimage?" (See the section marked "Pilgrimage Question," chapter 11.) Don't ask if he is a Christian. Often he will say "yes" and yet not have any understanding of the new birth. As you perceive his lack of understanding of the gospel, it then becomes necessary to prove that his affirmation (his "yes") was wrong.

Second, as he discusses his religious background, listen . . . carefully and patiently. Listen for understanding. When the opportunity comes to lead him to Christ, it is very helpful to know something of his background, beliefs, and experiences. By listening selectively, the evangelist notes key words which reveal, directly or indirectly, the person's objectives, needs, fears, and problems.

Listen for permission to continue the discussion. As you interact, note carefully his response. Although he may not verbally ask you to stop the conversation, the perceptive listener knows when the conversation is outside his present "comfort zone." Time and trust are the two keys to gradually stretching his spiritual comfort zone. Insensitivity at this point may close the door to any further discussion. Stretch him, yes, but not to the breaking point. Watch for signs of nervousness, wandering attention, a change of subject, or nonverbal evidences of hostility and resentment.

Third, eliminate caricatures of the gospel. This is one of the most important dimensions of seed planting. As the non-Christian contemplates the vast puzzle of Christianity, he visualizes a lot more pieces in it than Christ and the cross. Let me list a few of these distorting "pieces."

(1) "Christianity is keeping the golden rule. Therefore, for me to become a Christian, I must try harder." Hardly good news to someone who has tried and tried and failed and failed. To eliminate this caricature of the gospel, plant this thought. Just the other day my neighbor said to me, "I'm not a very religious person." I replied, "I'm not either. I was delighted to discover that Christianity isn't a religion, it's a relationship with a person, Jesus Christ." That to most non-Christians is a revolutionary thought. If you did nothing more than eliminate that caricature, you have made great progress in your evangelistic enterprise. It may be appropriate to stop the conversation at that point without pursuing it further. Believe me, the non-Christian who comes to understand just this one point has something to go home and think about. If you're his friend, he will!

(2)"To become a Christian I must give up everything that I enjoy." This is a partial truth. His observations have led him to conclude that Christians never have any fun. The caricature could be stated this way. "Christians are negative people; I don't want to be so negative, therefore, I don't want to be a Christian." Unfortunately, some Christians act in ways which reinforce the caricature. A super time at the beach can bury this caricature in a hurry—assuming you invite them. You can be the key to eliminating this distortion.

(3) "To become a Christian I must go to church and get involved in lots of meetings." This is the old "churchianity" caricature. Unfortunately, some of our churches perpetuate this idea by pushing a program which encourages a neurotic Christian activism. I shared with my neighbor that I wasn't interested in lots of meetings, but that I did enjoy regular times of *significant* teaching and worship. Obviously, the list of caricatures could go on and on. Take a paper and pencil and list a few of your own.

Caricatures are reasons for rejecting the gospel. As you plant seeds which gradually eliminate caricatures, you move the individual closer and closer to the cross. There are usually many "pre-decisions" which precede *the* decision. Elimination of caricatures predisposes the non-Christian towards making *the* decision. Each time the non-Christian has a caricature challenged, he faces a decision point. To reject a caricature is to remove one more excuse. If he discovers "Christians have more fun," he can no longer use the "no fun" caricature as an excuse. If he decides to reject the caricature, he has unknowingly taken a step towards the acceptance of Christ. The pre-decision decision has been made, and the nonbeliever moves one step closer to the cross. Believers must be very sensitive to the distortions of Christianity which exist in the nonbeliever's mind. At any given point, the believer's behavior either *reinforces* or *removes* these caricatures. BE a remover, not a reinforcer!

The fourth step to take as a seed planter is to highlight the positive aspects of the gospel. This you can do verbally and nonverbally. This involves all that we have said about how knowing Christ relates to various aspects of everyday life. "My wife and I have found that knowing Christ is a major key to our relationship as husband and wife." "Knowing Christ has given me a great peace of heart." "It's a wonderful thing to know that God has forgiven me for all my failures." Spread over a period of time, perceptive seed planting bears great fruit. It eventually leads you to the point of sharing the "words" of the gospel.

BE READY TO SHARE

The final key: *Be prepared to set the hook*. We do need to be able to share the *words* of the gospel. What a joy it is to introduce your friends to a saving knowledge of Jesus Christ. We will discuss how to personally share Christ in the final chapter.

Chapter 11

Your Personal Message of Evangelism

*I*t's time to share the "words" of the gospel. At this point, Christians are known to panic. They know the world's greatest, the world's most important, the world's most life-changing secret. And when its "time to tell," they choke. As ambassadors for Christ, they have the privilege of delivering the best news that any individual could possibly receive. It would seem that one of life's most fulfilling and sought after experiences would be sharing that good news. In reality, it's the one thing most Christians fear and avoid at all costs.

There are numerous reasons for such a response. Let me suggest two. Many Christians don't know *how* to share their faith. They have never disciplined themselves to learn a logical, biblical gospel presentation. A second hindrance is that many times the Christian doesn't know the person he is "evangelizing." As a result, the witnessing experience is often an embarrassment to both parties.

I have shared Christ on numerous occasions with virtual strangers and seen some of them respond. Praise the Lord for those who trust Christ under such circumstances! Unfortunately, only a small percentage of people become believers through such an encounter. Our goal is to mobilize the *majority* of believers to be involved in evangelism as a way of life. Natural, "organic" evangelism provides the most satisfying option for the largest number of believers. As a general rule, it is easier to share with a friend. And what a joyous occasion it proves to be. I often find tears of joy coursing down my cheeks as another friend trusts Christ. When have we come to the point in a relationship where it is appropriate to present the gospel and call for a decision? And what should we say when we do reach that point? In the next few pages I want to attempt to give you answers to those questions.

DETERMINING READINESS FOR THE GOSPEL

How do you know when you have reached this decision point? Let me answer this question by asking you some questions.

1. What do you know of the person's religious background?
2. What opportunities have you had to "plant seeds?" What was the response to these germinal ideas?
3. Do you sense that your neighbor enjoys being with you?
4. What needs have you discovered which relate to the gospel solution?
5. What caricatures have you been able to eliminate from his arsenal of questions and excuses?
6. What signs of openness have you detected?
   a. questions about religious things
   b. general freedom to discuss religious concepts
   c. openness to reading materials and other resources
   d. willing involvement in some harvest vehicles
   e. positive seeking attitude
7. How much of your personal testimony have you had a chance to share?

Obviously these questions are simply aids to help you come to a general feeling that the appropriate time has come. It is important that you be sensitive about timing. A familiar pledge among salesmen is illustrative. "I will not begin talking about my solution until I'm certain my prospect is eager to hear about it." Remember, it is the Spirit of God who convicts men of sin, righteousness, and judgment. The effective evangelist is in a cooperative relationship with God Himself. To be insensitive to or to fail to wait for evidences of the moving of the Spirit in the unbeliever's life is to hinder God's work.

THE PILGRIMAGE QUESTION

Let's assume that you feel your friend is getting close to a salvation decision point. You know something of his background, his needs, and the caricatures he embraces. What's next? Generally it is time to ask some key questions which "test the water." There is no "magic question," but I've found this one helpful. I call it my "pilgrimage question." "Bill, we've never had a chance to talk about your own religious background. At what point are you in your own spiritual pilgrimage?"

Notice a few insights concerning this question. First, it acknowledges the fact that coming to God involves a normal (but supernatural) process. Thus the individual feels that it is O.K. to still be in process.

The pilgrimage question does not ask whether one is a Christian or not. If asked that question, most people will say "yes" because they don't really understand what being a "Christian" is all about. Therefore your evangelism task becomes one of proving their "yes" answer to be wrong.

The pilgrimage question is general enough to allow a response without embarrassment. No one likes to be put on the spot. This question allows a person to choose a response appropriate to his own theological "comfort zone." His answer can be as simple or profound as he desires it to be.

The chief advantage of the pilgrimage question is the fact that it gives you one final time for spiritual appraisal. As you listen carefully to the response, you make the final decision as to whether or not to share the gospel of saving grace at this time.

The fact that you have allowed a person to share concerning his pilgrimage gives you a subtle advantage. It predisposes him to listen to you at the appropriate time. When you are ready to share the gospel, you want to do most of the talking. Let him talk first. Resist the temptation to jump into the conversation and deal with side issues. If he believes his church is the only true church offering the only true baptism producing the only true believers, don't debate the issue. Just listen! Affirm the truth of his *valid* insights, because you will soon have to challenge his viewpoint in some critical areas.

A related question is also helpful. "Has your spiritual pilgrimage come to the point of a personal commitment to Jesus Christ, or are you still on the way?" My experience has been that when people start talking about the present state of their spiritual pilgrimage you soon have all the information needed for the next step. I've had many respond to this "pilgrimage question" by saying "I'm still on the way." Great! At this point I'll usually say, "Well, Bill, maybe the next step God has for you is coming to understand how to establish a personal, saving relationship with Him."

Opportunity Statement

Because the purpose of the pilgrimage question is for him/her to pour out his/her religious beliefs, feelings, and concerns first, usually I find that little if any time will be left for me during this initial time period. Consequently, I plant seeds during our discussion time, designed to prepare for a later discussion. This we will call our "opportunity statement." I find it helpful to move from the pilgrimage question to this opportunity statement.

Here it is: *"Sometime I'd like the opportunity to share four principles which will enable you to understand what it means to establish a personal relationship with Christ."* A little later in the conversation I might reinforce the opportunity by saying, "Bill, I can identify with your rejection of religion, with all its formality and hypocrisy. When I get an opportunity to share those principles with you, they should help answer your questions in this area."

In some conversations I have dropped the idea of a further discussion five or six times. The response to this repeated suggestion must be observed and properly interpreted. It literally becomes your red or green light. At this point you may be thinking that such an approach is devious, humanistic, and unnecessary. On the contrary, the Bible teaches we are not to throw pearls to swine. Interpreted, the Lord is saying among other things that audience awareness is very important. He refused to perform miracles when he sensed hearts were hard. Sensitivity is what we are talking about. It is part of being "wise as serpents."

You can always count on this: As you get involved in discussing spiritual things, all the powers of hell itself go into operation to thwart your efforts. It is imperative that we be well-prepared, sharp instruments that the Spirit can use effectively and decisively. I am not suggesting a rote, mechanistic way of dealing with people. These are general principles which are to be adapted to specific, changing situations. No pilgrimage to God will involve all of these elements.

INTEREST QUESTION

As the initial discussion time closes, I've observed that it is helpful to change the opportunity statement into a question.

Pilgrimage Question:	At what point are you in your spiritual pilgrimage?
Opportunity Statement:	Sometime I'd like the opportunity to share four principles with you which will help you understand what it means to have a personal relationship with God.
Interest Question:	Could I share those four principles with you?

This polite offer now allows your listener to talk. It is his turn to respond.

SCHEDULE QUESTION

If the response is positive to the interest question ("Yes, I'd appreciate your sharing them," or "sounds great," etc.), schedule becomes the next focal point. Do you share the principles now or later? If later, some schedule-type questions are important.

"What's the best time for us to get together?"

"Is morning O.K. for you?"

"Is Wednesday or Friday better for you?"

"How about coming by my office (home, etc.) and we'll pursue this further?"

Once the agreed upon time is reached, . . . rejoice! Harvest is scheduled. A schooling fish has been identified, cultivated, and is about to take life's most important step! A new birth, a beginning as *new* as birth itself, is about to take place.

Opportunity Explanation

With a scheduled time and place, the next major focal point is the actual *opportunity explanation*. At this point the gospel itself (those four principles or whatever explanation of the gospel you prefer) is explained. The rest of the chapter following this analysis of the communication sequence will focus on how to summarize and present the gospel.

Decision Question

When the gospel is clearly set forth, the *decision questions* are the next logical step. Here we are simply asking the individual to personalize the truth. I usually find three questions to be helpful at this point.

1. Does this (the gospel) make sense to you?
2. On the basis of this (the gospel presentation) have you ever received Jesus Christ as your Savior?
3. Is there any reason why you wouldn't want to receive Jesus Christ right now?

Your friend is now at the point of decision. If he responds positively to the Spirit's wooing, he by faith will actualize the gospel opportunity and become a new creature in Christ.

The pilgrimage question is a spiritual litmus test. The opportunity statement is seed planting at its best (never underestimate the power of suggestion). It rouses curiosity and suggests a future course of action, a potential solution to some personal problems. The interest question is your way of determining whether or not your friend is open to and interested in pursuing conversation about those "four spiritual principles" (the gospel). Assuming he is, the schedule question puts a definite time frame into the decision making process. "Sometime" becomes next Tuesday at 8:00 a.m.! Then comes the gospel explanation, the decision questions, and the commitment to Christ!

Obviously, at any point in this communication sequence, the response could be negative. Your friend may go to the point of expressing an interest in hearing those mysterious "four principles," but may be hesitant when you start talking schedule. Don't panic. Praise God he's expressed a positive response to the idea of discussing spiritual things. Back off, continue to be his friend and wait for another opportunity. I actually had a neighbor call me up and say, almost in desperation, "Joe, you've *got* to share those principles with me." I did. He's now a brother in Christ. The following chart helps one see the options at each stage which are determined by the responses that are given.

- **Continuous Cultivation of a Growing, Deepening Relationship** ←

- **Pilgrimage Question:** "At what point are you . . . ?"
  POSITIVE RESPONSE   NEUTRAL/NEGATIVE RESPONSE

- **Opportunity Statement:** "Sometime I'd like the opportunity..."
  POSITIVE RESPONSE   NEUTRAL/NEGATIVE RESPONSE

- **Interest Question:** "Could I share those 4 principles with you?"
  POSITIVE RESPONSE   NEUTRAL/NEGATIVE RESPONSE

- **Schedule Question:** "What would be a good time for you?"
  POSITIVE RESPONSE   NEUTRAL/NEGATIVE RESPONSE

- **Opportunity Explanation:** Share the 4 principles.
  POSITIVE RESPONSE   NEUTRAL/NEGATIVE RESPONSE

- **Decision Questions:** "Is there any reason why you wouldn't receive Christ right now?
  POSITIVE RESPONSE   NEUTRAL/NEGATIVE RESPONSE

- **The Decision:** Accept Christ

- **Assurance and Follow-up**

Back off and continue developing the relationship

As a person approaches a decision for Christ, a major key at this point is confidence. Believe, indeed *expect,* the individual will trust the Lord. You've seen Him at work in your friend's life as you've spent time together. It's time to anticipate the rejoicing of angels in heaven! At this point, I fully expect God to bring the person to a point of salvation.

So, what do you do before your scheduled appointment? Begin by praying a lot. Although God uses human agency, it is God who draws people to Himself. But don't forget . . . He uses you. You are important to the process.

Then, if you haven't learned a good, logical, accurate gospel presentation, by all means learn one. At this point you may be saying "I don't like methods; I prefer to just trust the Spirit of God." The fallacy of this reasoning is that "no method" is a method. It's the "no method" method. It's the "hamburger in the fan" approach to effective communication. Certainly we do not harness the creative Holy Spirit with assembly line methodology. But the logical organization of the gospel essentials does not have to rule out creativity and diversity in presentation and emphasis.

I have presented the four spiritual laws hundreds of times and I'm sure the presentation has varied as to emphasis and content each time. Hopefully I adapt my presentation to the needs of the person I am sharing with. Granted, the great diversity in personality calls for a diversity in the way people are approached with the gospel. This fact, however, in no way rules out a carefully planned methodology.

The Holy Spirit puts no premium on lack of preparation or shoddy thinking. The Creator has designed our thinking process to follow certain rational patterns of communication to logical conclusions. A disorganized, haphazard, illogical gospel presentation violates both natural and spiritual laws. Whatever else may be said, God is not the author of confusion. On the other hand, logic, brilliance, or the "powers of persuasion" are not to be a substitute for the Spirit. A carefully thought through presentation communicates to the listener that the message is important and worthy of his attention. What are the characteristics of a good method? I will suggest a few.

1. Biblically accurate and balanced
2. Logical in its development with good transitions between its major points
3. Clear in its content, avoiding churchy, unfamiliar language

4. Clear in its intent, with no question about the action steps necessary for the individual to receive Christ
5. Positive in its basic content, reflecting the reality that the gospel is "good news"
6. Simple rather than complex
7. Attractive in format, meaning a well-designed, quality piece of literature if printed

PRINCIPLES FOR A PERSONAL GOSPEL PRESENTATION

Before looking at the actual sharing process, I'd like to consider some foundational communication principles.

In sharing the gospel, we are actually *converting biblical facts into people benefits*. Jesus did not come to condemn the world. Keep this in mind as you share the good news. Justification, translated into modern terminology, offers incredible people benefits. Besides being God's provision to deliver me from judgment, it is the key to deliverance from guilt with all its interpersonal ramifications. The indwelling Christ is the answer to the powerlessness and futility of the nonbeliever's everyday existence. Highlight these benefits.

The effective evangelist works towards *establishing a supportive, nourishing climate for communication*. Only seven percent of effective communication is verbal, thirty-eight percent is tone of voice, and fifty-five percent is totally nonverbal. If you establish a defensive environment, the unbeliever will spend most of his time trying to guard himself against both you and your message. Eliminate your holy hush, stained-glass voice or your religious twang. You are not a judge or a jury either. You are a sinner showing another sinner how to draw water from the well of life. A caring, sensitive manner is vital for sharing the good news. If you view this sharing process as a contest between you and the prospective believer, this value judgment will be reflected in your attitude, tone, and behavior. The unbeliever is not an enemy and the evangelist must not seek a decision in this battleground framework. If "victory at all costs" is what we value, this attitude will vitally influence the way in which we relate to others. The goal is to win friends, not arguments. Evangelism is not something the Christian does *to* an unbeliever as an object. Sharing Christ is something a believer does *with* an unbeliever as his friend, confidant, and guide.

The effective evangelist *communicates empathy by asking questions and listening carefully*. Empathy is the ability to become a naturalized citizen of another person's world. The effective evangelist uses empathy to help discover the unbeliever's problems and devise precise gospel solutions. Generally, people are not afraid to believe, but they are afraid of being "sold." Questions are necessary diagnostic tools because people only hear answers to the questions they are asking. Communication is not complete until the recipient hears with understanding. Our questions not only help us uncover their questions and concerns, but they convey the fact that we care. Used as diagnostic tools, well-designed questions help develop tension between what is and what ought to be. Spirit-directed questions can build conviction (tension) which in turn moves the unbeliever towards seeking the gospel solution. By listening carefully and using questions skillfully, the evangelist communicates empathy.

I have found that questions are used most effectively in the early stages of sharing the gospel. They become tools to aid discussion and seek "pilgrimage status" information. As a general rule, the more questions have been used in the early states of the evangelism process, the less they are needed when it is appropriate to share the words of the gospel. Key questions may be asked *months* before the actual gospel presentation. This helps the actual presentation because the unbeliever has already had his "day in court." He has had an opportunity to share his beliefs and voice his opinions. Now it is your turn to talk, and because you have listened and used questions wisely, your gospel presentation has added impact.

Effective communications are marked by humility and gentleness. If you don't know the answer to a question, admit it. Don't assume the "I know everything" attitude. The goal is not to smother the unbeliever with facts. Often we try to communicate too much too fast.

Effective evangelists eliminate everything which is offensive (other than the offense of the cross itself). Bad breath, unkempt clothes, body odor, and poor personal hygiene are inexcusable. Such considerations as lighting, ventilation, and privacy while not "gospel essentials" should not be overlooked. Not to be sensitive to the unbeliever's time schedule is also wrong. Be on time, and finish at the appropriate time.

Let's assume you are with your friend, and are ready to move from the normal "small talk" to spiritual things. The following suggestions are just that: suggestions. You will have to develop a gospel presentation which is comfortable to you.

A Transition

The first challenge you face is to change the conversation to spiritual things. A good transition is the key. Campus Crusade for Christ has one I use quite often. "Just as there are physical laws which govern the physical universe, there are spiritual laws which govern our relationship with God. Bill, I'd like to share four of these principles with you." I often explain that whether or not I believe in the law of gravity, if I jump off a building, I'll become a believer. Recognition doesn't determine reality. Whether I recognize it or not, our universe is controlled by physical and spiritual laws. My denial of these facts does not change the reality of them.

Paper and Pencil

I prefer to actually write out the four laws (basics of the gospel) on a piece of paper. There are many advantages to this. First, it is more personal than reading from a booklet. Second, it focuses attention on what you are doing. Third, it enables you to "personalize your presentation." You can add extra charts, diagrams, or illustrations. Fourth, you can give the sheet to them when you're finished with it. If you don't, most people will ask you for it. It becomes a precious document, a sort of "birth certificate" for many of them. I've had people open their Bibles and show me their "certificate" years after I shared Christ with them. In a Madison Avenue world with prepackaged everything it's nice to add a personal touch (assuming your writing is legible).

Hold the Questions

This is your time to share. You've allowed your friend to share his pilgrimage. You've asked questions and listened carefully. If a question comes up, compliment the question. "Bill, that's a very perceptive question." Instead of interrupting the train of thought with an answer, make a suggestion. "Bill, would it be O.K. to hold that question until I have finished sharing the rest of these principles? I believe your question will be answered. If not, I'd be happy to respond to it." A deferred question seldom comes up again when the essence of the gospel has been clearly presented. Obviously it is sometimes impossible (and unwise) to defer a question. If that is the case, answer it briefly and move on.

Read or Quote the Pertinent Scripture Verses

The Word is quick and powerful. Use it. If it is possible, let your friend actually look on with you as you read. It will be a great joy to you as you actually experience the Spirit of God using His Holy Word to direct people to Jesus Christ. I would guard against using too much Scripture. Once you have made your point, move on.

Plant Seeds Again

I like to suggest the appropriate and expected action that needs to be taken several times during the gospel presentation. "Bill, *when* you make a commitment to Christ, you will discover what it means to have the peace of God." "*When* you receive Christ you will find that God will enable you to grow in your family relationship." "When Christ becomes part of your life, the God-shaped vacuum in your life will be filled . . .", etc. This lets your friend know what the appropriate and expected action is. It conveys confidence on your part that he both needs to make this decision and that he will. Our verbal (semantic) message needs to be backed up by our nonverbal message. If we convey fear, uncertainty and tentativeness nonverbally, our friend is receiving contradictory messages.

It is reasonable to expect a favorable response. Having cultivated a friendship and bathed it in prayer, what else should we expect? Are the fields white or not? When you're standing knee-deep in a white field why be hesitant? Too many Christians, like the proverbial ostriches, go bury their heads . . . in the grain. Suggesting the action step several times also prepares the person for the coming call to commitment. On numerous occasions the individual is so prepared by God that I've actually had him ask, "Well, how do I receive Him?" before I've finished the presentation.

Another advantage to this "when you . . ." type of seed planting is that it builds your own confidence. For most Christians the hardest part of sharing the gospel is calling for a commitment. Seed planting makes it easier and less threatening to transition to this vital part of the gospel.

Share Analogous Examples

Analogous examples are "if the shoe fits, wear it" types. Because you know some of your friend's needs, you can share illustrations of others with similar needs who found a solution in Christ. Suppose Bill has difficulty expressing love and affection and you have seen him struggle in this area. Without making reference to his need, you might comment, "Bill, a friend of mine whose marriage was in trouble came and shared his concerns. I shared with him that a relationship with Christ could make a significant difference. He received Christ and found that things began to change. He hasn't solved all the problems yet, but has found renewed hope. When you receive Christ I believe you will be delighted to see the changes He will make in your own life."

Share Personal Experiences

Avoid the old "before Christ I was a revolting rat and now I'm a super saint" mentality. At best, only half of the statement is true. Authenticity at this point is important. Avoid all temptations to "pump sunshine." Progress that you have made is appropriate information to share. But don't leave the impression that you have arrived. You haven't (your pastors haven't, either). The fact that you are progressing towards a *destination* is good news to many. If they're really friends they've already seen you spill your milk.

Experiences which they can identify with are especially valuable. If the individual is struggling with the issue of trusting Christ, share your personal fears and apprehensions as you approached this decision point (assuming you had them).

Be Natural

I can't stress this enough. Relax. God draws people to Himself . . . through you. Guard against getting "hyper" (a favorite word of my son). This doesn't mean you need to be Cool Hand Luke. Be yourself and talk (not preach, manipulate, or coerce) with your friend. I am in no way suggesting that you be solemn or sanctimonious. Humor can be very effective as a tension reliever. Use it wisely. Tears? Why not. This is a joyous occasion. I often find myself shedding tears of joy. A prodigal son is coming home. Glory!

Use Repetition and Review for Impact

Regardless of the plan you use, when you have finished one point, review it and move on to the next one. "Bill, up to this point, we've seen that God really does love you. You are special to Him." When you move on to a third major point, quickly review the other two. This reinforces the truth and increases understanding.

Adapt Your Presentation to His Needs

If because of extreme guilt and insecurity the individual needs reassurance of God's love, spend more time making this point. If he is already broken by sin, don't belabor the issue. The person who knows little about Christ may need you to share some critical insights about His uniqueness. It may be necessary to spend most of your time discussing His person and work. For others who you sense understand Christ's uniqueness but have never responded to Him perhaps most of your focus needs to be on the need to receive Him as Savior. Sometimes this adaptation takes the form of quotations and comments from notable scholars and leaders. These can be powerful. Start collecting and memorizing them. I have memorized quotes about Jesus Christ from many notable historical figures. They are especially effective for the individual struggling with the intellectual integrity of a commitment to Christ. Josh McDowell's book, *Evidence that Demands a Verdict,* is full of valuable quotes.

Present the Opportunity to Trust Christ

The time has come to seek a commitment. The Decision Questions provide a helpful way to make this an effective, productive experience.

1. Does this make sense?
2. On the basis of this, have you ever committed your life to Christ?
3. Is there any reason why you would not want to trust Christ right now?

The first question helps you know whether or not your friend understands the basic gospel presentation. The second question provides you with your friend's evaluation of his relationship to Jesus Christ. The third question is particularly important. Note that it does not ask if the person wants to receive Christ. This question would anticipate a "yes or no" answer. Instead, it asks if there is a *reason* why the unbeliever would not want to trust Christ. At this point, you anticipate his fear. As you mention praying to receive Christ many non-Christians panic. They haven't done much praying and fear embarrassment. I've found this to be helpful: "Bill, I've shared Christ with many people, and I've found they sometimes feel awkward praying. I can appreciate that, even though the words are not important. God knows your heart. If it makes sense to you, why don't I pray out loud, and if what I pray expresses how you feel, why don't you pray out loud after me. Does this make sense?" If so, I usually lead in prayer, one phrase at a time. Often the individual adds comments of his own. These are precious moments. What a joy to lead your friend to Christ.

Provide Assurance and Follow-up

Most gospel presentations have some simple thoughts to assure the individual of the reality of the new birth. I will not repeat them. Follow-up is a delight because friends enjoy being together. Again, there are many helpful follow-up books available. Check with your pastor for a suitable one.

Where do you go from here? To the beauty parlor, of course. From there it is out to love a friend to Christ. You'll never have time if I keep writing. I'll quit writing about evangelism so you can start doing it . . . beautifully. See you in glory. Introduce me to your neighbors when we get there. By God's grace you'll meet some of mine.

Scripture Index

Subject Index

Abraham, 167, 168, 170
Absolutes, 55
Accardy, Frank, 149
Acceptance, 193
Accountability, 119, 163
Adam, 125
Adaptation of Gospel presentation, 233
Alienation, 18, 86
Altar call, 117-118
"Ambush" method, 20
Anti-supernaturalism, 127
Aquarium, stained glass, 19, 174
Aristotle, 35
Assimilation, 65
Assurance, 234
Atmosphere, 190-194
Attitude, 111, 202
Authenticity, 126-127, 135, 153, 172-173

Balance, 63, 171
Beauty
  as effective witness, 28, 36
  as purpose of Christ's love, 26
  as result of God's love, 28
  as result of unity, 135
  death of, 46
  definition of, 29
  in evangelistic Bible studies, 190
  in God's evangelism strategy, 23
Believer, 27-28, 33, 106-113
Bible studies, evangelistic, 187-199
Bible study, for pastors, 173
Blamelessness, 27
Body of Christ. *See* Church
Bonhoeffer, Dietrich, 86
Books, giving, 210-211
Bride
  as displayer of God, 36, 67
  as God's strategy for evangelism, 25-26
  edification of, 121
  impurity as destroyer of, 130

Bright, Bill, 129

Campus Crusade for Christ, 129, 230
Campus Life magazine, 211
Caricatures of Christianity, 215-216
Christian Life magazine, 211
Church
  as a community, 106-113, 120-121
  as a healing communion, 118-120
  as a learning center, 116-118
  board, 143, 155
  characteristics of, 116-123
  discipline, 130-131
  evangelism, 22, 80, 104-105
  health of, 102-104
  hypocrisy in, 126-127
  impact on non-believers, 109
  in the community, 176-177
  leadership, 142-144
  ministry focus of, 127
  nature of, 26, 83, 104
  product of, 105-106, 115-116
  programs, 108, 117, 120, 174
  reaction to impurity, 130-131
  service of, 121-123
"Churchianity", 216
Cliches, 190
Common interests with non-Christians. *See* Interests, common
Communication, 228-230, 231
Communicator, characteristics of, 35
Community. *See* Church as a community
Compromise, 55
Conceit in a new convert, 149
Confession, 127
Confidence, 226
Conformity, 53-54
Conscience, 52-53, 62-63, 70-71, 124
Context of evangelism, 20, 190
Controversy, 47

241